WATERLINES

WRITING LESSONS FROM A LIFE AFLOAT

CRAFT, CREATIVITY AND THE WRITING LIFE
BOOK 1

RICHARD BEYNON

HOT TYPE PRESS

Waterlines: Writing Lessons from a Life Afloat
Craft, Creativity and the Writing Life Book 1

www.richardbeynonbooks.com

Paperback ISBN: 978-1-918023-01-5
Ebook ISBN: 978-1-918023-00-8
Workbook ISBN: 978-1-918023-02-2

For permissions or rights inquiries, please contact:
rich@richardbeynonbooks.com

Book design by Nuno Moreira, NM DESIGN

Published by Hot Type Press

For Trish

COMES PERPETUA

CONTENTS

The water does not resist. Water flows. When you plunge your hand into it, all you feel is a caress. - *Margaret Atwood*

IN THE BEGINNING

I spent a year in hospital after an encounter with polio back in the mid-Fifties, just before the Salk vaccine became widely available. Part of my rehabilitation involved physio sessions in the indoor pool.

I was seven, and I had just been fitted with my first caliper – an elaborate device replete with straps around my waist, my thigh, my knee and my calf, all secured with small metal buckles. Putting it on was a long, exhausting business and, frankly, by the time I'd done it a dozen or more times, it was boring.

Now, I had begun consuming the children's books in our ward. I was, as far as I knew, the only boy on the ward who read anything but comics. It struck me, sitting in my cubicle after half an hour's exercise in the pool, and contemplating the metal and leather monstrosity beside me, that I had a bargaining chip to play.

"If you help me put on my caliper," I told Walter, a boy with cerebral palsy who shared my cubicle, "I'll tell you a story."

He regarded me suspiciously. "What sort of story?"

"A story about pirates and buried treasure," I said, drawing freely on the book I'd begun the evening before. Walter did a quick cost-benefit analysis of my proposition and nodded.

"Okay," he said, "long as it's exciting."

I positioned my leg in the caliper and gestured for him to begin. "Once upon a time," I said, "there was a famous pirate called Blackbeard..."

For the next several months, until, in fact, I was discharged, I told Walter and a number of other boys with whom I shared my physio sessions a series of stories. And as my facility at retailing stories grew, so did their skill at strapping me into my caliper.

The experience taught me two things: one, that stories had real value, and two, that I had some skill at telling them. Of course, they weren't *my* stories. But I was aware that I was elaborating on them, changing their endings in some cases, giving characters names of my choosing.

A great many writers attribute their urge to write to an early encounter with books, or, in many cases, a single book that had a singular impact on their imaginations.

My discovery that between the covers of the books on the shelf in our ward lay entire worlds, populated with characters both admirably virtuous and deliciously wicked was the incident that incited my love affair both with reading and writing. It's a passion that can be traced from the day I read my first big book – Enid Blyton's *Castle of Adventure*, as it happens – to the publication of this book.

But before we go any further, there's a second passion I have to confess.

Let's skip ahead many years, to 2006 when my wife, Trish, her children, Maria and Jamie, and I set off from our mooring in Newark, a brand new 43 HP Nanni engine purring under the rear deck of a narrowboat, heading for a slot we'd secured in a marina in central Birmingham.

Why a narrowboat? Why a boat at all, for that matter? Here's the confession:

As a child, fresh out of that rehabilitation hospital and now firmly and irrevocably addicted to reading, I'd ploughed through *The Wind in the Willows,* and, later, Arthur Ransome's sequence of novels detailing the adventures of the groups of children called the Swallows and Amazons. They'd sailed on Windermere, the Broads, and the North Sea.

I'd fallen in love with the idea of boats. And then, after I was able to translate my fantasies into action, not on a vast lake, but a narrow, sinuous river called the Klip south of Johannesburg, and not in a sailing dinghy, but a canoe, I agreed wholeheartedly with Ratty when he solemnly declared to his new friend Mole that "there is nothing – absolutely nothing – half so much worth doing as simply messing about in boats."

Later, as a student at Leeds University, I'd noticed narrowboats plying the local canals, and swore that one day I too would set sail on one of my own.

So, Trish and I invested our savings in a fifty-foot narrowboat called Patience. The engine was new – but the boat was ten years old.

For the next twelve years, often accompanied by one of our children, we came from South Africa every year to spend a month or two or more to cruise the waterways of England and Wales.

We were able to manage this perpetual juggling act because we were both freelancers. Trish was a production designer and art director of film and television, and I was a writer of drama and comedy for television.

In the year we acquired Patience, with a novelist friend, Jo-Anne Richards, we established a company teaching creative writing called All About Writing, which operated, for the most part, even in those pre-pandemic times, online. So, it was entirely possible to take prolonged working holidays. I spent part of most days writing television and film scripts – my day job - and assessing assignments that our students submitted online, while Trish administered and marketed our writing courses.

We crossed the country, going as far as Llangollen in the west, up to Manchester and Wigan, across the Pennines to Leeds, and back down the River Trent.

We changed our home base from Birmingham to Braunston, once the hub of the waterways, now a quiet village just south of Rugby.

We cruised from Braunston to Oxford via canal, and then up the Thames to as far as it's possible to navigate, at Lechlade, before turning and steaming down river to London, passing a group of Swan Uppers en route, and a grand and gilded flotilla of riverboats marking the Queen's Diamond Jubilee.

We criss-crossed London several times and repeatedly made the trip between Paddington Basin, tucked in behind the station, and Braunston, (100 miles and 90 heavy double locks).

We explored the River Nene down to Peterborough, crossed through what is called the Middle Levels to the River Great Ouse, and powered all the way up to the limits of its navigation just beyond Bedford.

But seven years ago, we decided to switch moorings again. That final voyage had persuaded us that Bedford offered a number of highly desirable features: a beautiful section of the river, moorings on a lake with a community of boaters and easy access to London – it's just 41 minutes on the fast train to St Pancras.

In 2011, a year or two after we'd moved Patience to Braunston, Trish asked me to write a weekly blog for our online community.

"What sort of blog?" I was a little suspicious. A weekly blog seemed like an arduous undertaking.

"I don't know," she said. "Something inspiring. About writing, you know."

"I thought it might be about something interesting like pig-keeping."

"I hate it when you're sarcastic."

After I agreed to drop my scepticism, we settled on a general theme of motivation, stimulation and inspiration. I thought of what I might write as little meditations. And because I'd written a great many sitcom scripts, I imagined I'd be able to inject the occasional note of humour too.

So I sat myself down at the desk in Patience's saloon, looked out at the fleet of narrowboats at anchor in the marina, and thoughtfully chewed my pencil. I needed something to get writers off their arses and in front of their writing desks, pen in hand, or keyboard at the ready. But they should do this because they wanted to. Writing had always been – and should always be – satisfying and fun, even when it is difficult and the words have to be squeezed out like the last half inch of toothpaste from an exhausted tube.

It occurred to me that writing is, above all else, a solitary pursuit – but that, on your writing journey, you're surrounded by the creations of your own imagination. "It's precisely *because* we're able to create entire worlds and a cast of thousands," I wrote, "and then set them off on journeys to Mt Doom or the Land of Oz, that we're never entirely alone."

That first blog was a little awkward, a little muddled, but it was mine own. Having composed it, I turned to Trish.

"What should we call it?"

"I don't know. You choose."

"How about Monday Motivations?" I'd always been a sucker for alliteration.

"Good. Every Monday."

I've more or less kept to that demanding schedule ever since – with breaks for the occasional holiday and bout of illness. So far I've written about six hundred of them. They're intended, as Trish and I decided initially, to offer a sometimes humorous, sometimes wry, sometimes inspiring look at the challenges that writers of all kinds face. Above all, they're intended to move people to pursue the dream of writing. They in turn have often been inspired by books and articles I've read or listened to; by films I've seen; by events I've attended; and above all by the incidents that have occurred on our journeys by water.

Hence the umbrella title of this series: *Craft, Creativity and the Writing Life.*

This book is a collection of my writing inspired by the waters we've cruised. The volumes that will follow it are less literally water-based, but are, in a sense, all water-logged in some deep way. Water, I've come to think, is a writer's medium: transparent, mysterious, lively and deep. But those volumes are arranged in such a way as to focus your attention on the different formal elements of creative writing: characters, story, dialogue and so on.

But let me be clear about something: neither this book, nor the volumes to come, are formal lessons in writing; and they don't add up to a comprehensive treatment of any of the subjects I touch on. Instead, they are inspirations conjured into life by my experiences – many of them on water – which have helped readers overcome their own demons, identify their own inspirations and motivated them to dive into their own creativity.

1

FIRST VOYAGE

BRAUNSTON TO OXFORD

THE STORY OF ABIGAIL

We returned to our narrowboat Patience this week and found on the foredeck, neatly deposited within the bounds of the lifebuoy we keep in case of aquatic misadventure, ten ivory-coloured eggs.

One was broken, spilling out its deep yellow yolk onto the deck.

There was no sign of the bird that had laid the eggs. We scraped away the yolk and tossed it and the shell into the murky waters of the marina in which we moor Patience and, imagining that the clutch had been abandoned, we carefully transferred the eggs from the deck to a container, which we left in the sun on the deck.

I was all for whipping a couple of them up into an omelette. "Two'd do it," I told Trish. "They're bloody big eggs."

In fact, a mallard's eggs on average are no larger than a hen's – but these were bigger than that, each easily filling my palm.

But Trish would have none of it. "The mother could be hanging about waiting to see what's become of her eggs."

"I think she's a delinquent mum. We should take them into care."

"Making omelettes out of them doesn't sound very caring at all," Trish said.

I would have pressed my case a little further but for the fact that, right at that moment, we heard peeping and chirping sounds of evident distress coming from the bow. We opened the doors and surprised a large and discombobulated mallard duck standing next to the bowl of eggs. Her name quite obviously was Abigail.

Consternation on Patience. What to do? Finally we settled on transferring the eggs into a large shallow dish and placing it in the lifebuoy. Of course, Abigail leapt from the prow in alarm when we emerged from the saloon to do this. We retreated into the boat and watched.

A minute later Abigail returned, stood beside her brood and regarded our handiwork with deep suspicion. After some minutes, however, instinct overcame whatever hesitation our interference had caused, and she settled on her eggs, whoomphing out her feathers to cover every last one of the nine survivors.

We watched from the confines of the saloon. Abigail made small, contented noises which triggered in us, respectively, a sense of paternal and maternal duty done. We'd saved Abigail's brood.

Now, what, you might ask, has this little slice of natural history to do with writing? Well, watching Abigail purr atop her clutch of eggs, a metaphor sprang to mind that seems singularly instructive.

We all give birth to ideas. For most of us, most of the time, those ideas are as ephemeral as the mist on a chilly morning in the marina. Like dreams, they evaporate, and just hours later we have no real memory of them at all. Damn, we say, I wish I could remember that thought I had. It had real promise.

If we're wise and, even more important, diligent, we write those ideas down. We ponder them. We turn them this way and that. We *incubate* them. Some, no doubt, will never hatch. But if we're faithful, if we've paid attention to the possibilities inherent in them, if we warm them and nurture them, if we *love* them – then those ideas will grow wings and fly.

So, there's the lesson Abigail can teach us. It's a simple one, but it's an important one.

Right, now, though, I need to put metaphor aside and return to the real Abigail and her prodigious output (although Mr Google tells me mallard clutches range between eight and thirteen eggs, and that their combined weight is half the poor mother's).

Abigail proved to be a flighty parent. During the first night of our return, she sat her eggs with admirable scrupulousness. The next morning, however, she took some hours off to fraternise with a friendly drake.

And now, on the evening of our second day, there is no sign of her. Her eggs lie cold and abandoned on our prow. There is no hope of them ever hatching.

I still think they'd make splendid omelettes, or even a vast frittata, but Trish will have none of it. Her argument has changed, however.

"How do we know that the little embryos aren't half formed inside the eggs? Imagine how ghastly it'd be if we cracked them open and found *embryos* inside. Like so many still-births."

It was a potent point, and I desisted.

"Besides," she added, "even if the eggs were still, you know, *eggs*, it would be like eating the offspring of a friend."

P.S. Newsflash: While Abigail was gallivanting, a beady-eyed crow alighted on our prow and scoffed all the eggs. See what happens to ideas when you don't properly attend to them?

WRITING IS THE SEA WE SWIM IN

We've hit a lucky summer. We've been back on Patience for a week now, and the warm weather has persisted. Our plan is to abandon our narrowboat to the tender care of David Bishop, a specialist boat painter, to repaint her. It'll take him a week or two to strip her down to bare metal (sounds cruel, I know, but it must be done) and then give her, I think he told us, five separate licks of paint. He tells us that he's employed an even more specialist painter of letters to inscribe Patience's name, and origin, in suitably elegant style.

Trish – in a previous, pre-Patience life, she was an art director for film and television – has settled on a deep green for the sides, and cream for the top.

In the few days we have before the painting's to begin, we're enjoying the weather, and getting reacquainted with Patience and her many quirks.

All around us lie a fleet of other narrowboats: Patricia and Star, Bess and Syren, Birdsong and Slow Gin. A construction vehicle trundles up and down the road just beyond the end of our jetty, carrying who knows what from somewhere to elsewhere.

We'll be on Patience for the next six months. It used to be that we came for the English summers, returning to Johannesburg once the cold there had lost its bitter edge. But this year we're here until the end of January, so we'll find out in due course how well we hold up to sleet and snow within the confines of our little world.

Patience is, like all narrowboats, high on romance and low on space. She boasts a long saloon, a small but more than adequate kitchen, a shower and loo, and a cabin with a standard double bed.

In the saloon we've found room for two bookshelves on which we've accumulated a range of novels, maps, canal guides and books on writing.

And that's what I'd like to talk about today. The first of the five books on writing is one called *Object Lessons: the Paris Review presents the art of the short story.* It features twenty great short stories introduced by twenty distinguished writers. I've only read a couple so far, but the insights offered by the commentators are excellent. I must read it all before our workshop in Stow in September where our subject is story.

The second is a rather more practical volume devoted to the tricky business less of writing than of publishing what you've written. *From Pitch to Publication*, it's called, with an explanatory sub-title: *Everything You Need To Know To Get Your Novel Published.* It's by Carole Blake, now sadly dead, but in her day one of the more formidable of Britain's battalion of literary agents.

The third is James Wood's *The Fun Stuff and other essays.* James Wood is a staff writer on the *New Yorker,* and Professor of the Practice of Literary Criticism at Harvard. A more astute critic and literary analyst (with barrel-loads of advice for any practising writer) I have yet to encounter. These essays appeared in various prestigious literary magazines, including *The New Yorker*, and tackle, sometimes devastatingly, a range of books and writers. There are no holy cows in James Wood's pantheon. Writing, for instance, of a character in a Paul Auster novel, Wood says: "He is supposed to be a dreamy young poet, but is half in love with easeful cliché." Ouch. And a little later: "At times, the prose seems to be involved in some weird, breathless competition to fit the greatest number of shop-worn objects into its basket..."

The fourth is a new one, which I have not yet opened, by Oliver Tearle: *Britain by the Book – a curious tour of our literary landscape.* It's a compendium of literary tales and anecdotes which resembles, in some little way, the meandering journeys we take in Patience.

And finally, there's Julia Cameron (author, remember, of *The Artist's Way)* and her book, *The Right to Write: An Invitation and Initiation into the Writing Life.* It's also a collection of essays. Let me quote the opening paragraph of the essay called *This Writing Life*:

> Outside the study window, the horses are cued* up waiting for me to feed them their breakfast. They are hungry and cranky – the way I feel when I don't write. For me, writing is an appetite, a joy. Even when I don't think I want it, even when I think I have nothing to say, it seduces me like the first really balmy day of spring: I want out of whatever I am doing and into it.

Writing is more than putting words on the page or screen. It's also about immersing yourself in the craft, about learning tips and reading insights that other writers have to offer or in admiring the skill of a fellow writer who manages to accomplish something with words that has defeated you.

Writing (and reading) is the sea we swim in, and, just as explorers read the accounts that other adventurers have written about their journeys, so we writers should revel in the maps and guides that other writers have produced about the journeys *they* have undertaken.

So looking now at our two modest shelves of books, I realise that the row of canal guide books are not, after all, very different from the five books we have on writing.

Each is an invitation and an inspiration. They've already inspired us to make, with Maria, my step-daughter, a mammoth three-month trip that took us to Manchester, Wigan, Leeds and Lincoln.

In the same way, each of the books on writing – and there are very many more back in my study in Johannesburg – is capable of inspiring a journey of a very different kind.

* Cued or Queued? Now more than ever, I recognise the accuracy of Winston Churchill's observation (and G.B. Shaw's before him) that "Americans and British are one people separated by a common language."

THE NAMES WE CALL EACH OTHER

Good morning, Nancy... Using your first name suggests a certain degree of intimacy. If instead I addressed you more formally, as Mr or Mrs or Prof or Ms Pottermack, then that would suggest a different kind of relationship... Or it would imply that on this occasion, at least, I wanted to keep things on a more, shall we say, professional level.

If on the other hand, I addressed you as "Shrimp", or "Bunny", or "Fatty", or "The Rooster", I would be exploiting the freedom that only a shared history, or a malicious desire to insult and demean you, gave me.

Our canalboat, Patience is propped up on great wooden wedges on the floor of Braunston Marina's drydock and, so far, David Bishop, the painter – I introduced him to you in the last piece – has spent all his time stripping layer after layer of flaking paint away. Patience is ten years old, and I doubt she's had more than one, her original, paint job.

David is a personable individual, with an impeccable reputation. He's not excessively young, which is to say he doesn't necessarily have to address me in formal, respectful terms. But I observe that he insists on, and persists in, calling me Mr Beynon, despite my having urged him on two or three occasions, to call me by my first name.

In doing this, he maintains what he believes is the correct distance from me. He is, after all, engaged by me to do a job of work. Until it's completed to my satisfaction, my guess is that he'll go on addressing me as Mr. I'm fascinated to see whether, when the work is done, and I suggest we have a Hooky (that's the fabulous ale brewed thirty miles or so to the southwest in the Cotswold village of Hook Norton) he relaxes sufficiently to call me Richard.

In Russia, as well as your first and last names, every individual, as I understand it, also boasts a patronymic – a name that points to his or her forebears. Wikipedia explains it like this:

> A patronymic is a component of a personal name based on the given name of one's father, grandfather, or an even-earlier male ancestor. A component of a name based on the name of one's mother or a female ancestor is a matronymic. Each is a means of conveying lineage.

From my reading of Russian literature, it seems to me that respect – and, in different circumstances, intimacy – can be signified by the use, in conversation, of the patronymic.

In French, whether to use "tu" or "vous" is a perennial and complex problem involving the desire to suggest intimacy, class status and one's acknowledged place in the hierarchy. Pretty nifty.

In English, we don't have the same means with which to signify all these subtleties.

But we do have the various forms of address I've touched on above.

And I haven't even mentioned all the other tools we have at our disposal. Words like "sir", "captain", "chief", as well as words of absolute derision and insult.

So consider these examples. In each a different person addresses the same Dr Alexander "Bugs" Featherstonehaugh:

"Hi, Bugs."

"Good morning, Dr F."

"Alex, darling, zip me up, please."

"Doctor, I have a pain here."

"Whatcha doing after work today, doc?"

"Watch your step, Mr Featherstonehaugh, sir."

Now guess to whom these various sentences could be attributed.

There are a number of clues, of course – but chief amongst them, I'd suggest, are the various ways in which they address the good doctor.

I've worked on television productions where over the years, writers became more and more lax about the ways in which different characters address each other – and ended up in the invidious position where everyone called everyone else by their first names.

The point is a simple one. When one of your characters addresses another, think a moment about the social, hierarchical, sexual and other implications of the name and title they might use. It sends a message to the alert reader.

When we took delivery of our newly painted Patience, I extended a hand to David.

"It looks fantastic."

"Not a bad job," he said, casting a critical eye over his handiwork.

"Up to you now, Mr Beynon, to keep her looking good."

"Got a little time for a Hooky up at the Nelson?"

"Oh, sorry. I've got an appointment with another owner. Sixty-footer. Wide-beam. Can't afford to be late for that."

He tipped his hat, fired a final, "Goodbye, Mr Beynon", and was off.

IT'S SENSATIONAL

This is going to be a deeply subjective missive – although, I suppose, there's an argument to say that every one of these pieces is deeply subjective: how could they not be?

The journey from Braunston to Oxford takes a little less than an hour and a half by road. By canal, it takes a little longer.

Consider: you travel southwest along the Grand Union for a few miles to Wigrams Turn, which marks the intersection of the Grand Union with the South Oxford Canal, a meandering section that runs through the bucolic countryside of Oxfordshire. It was built in the 1770s and '80s by James Brindley. To avoid having to build locks - they're the expensive bits of any canal – he'd followed the contours of the landscape, so for long miles we could putter along and contemplate, at two and a half miles an hour, the slowly changing vistas on either side.

So tortuously does the canal snake through the countryside, that a prominent radio mast shifts position in relation to your boat from side to side, from back to front and back again.

Four days after leaving Braunston, we've moored at the visitors' moorings in Banbury, alongside the Red Café, which is itself attached to the Banbury Museum. We face the prospect of another full days cruising to get to our destination. It's no wonder that one of the slogans frequently uttered by narrowboaters on the canals, with an air of quiet, not to say smug, satisfaction, is: Cruising on canals offers you the fastest way to slow down.

All that time sitting at the tiller has inspired a whole series of thoughts and reflections.

The thought I'd like to explore is hardly a thought at all: it's a sensation or, rather, a string of sensations. I cast my mind back to our journey...

I'm sitting at the tiller. Beneath my feet, beneath the deck, our four-stroke Nanni diesel engine thrums, a constant sensory accompaniment to all that follows.

Sometimes sunlight glints off the richly coloured water. A little later wildly swirling gusts tear at the hawthorn hedgerow running along the tow path. Later still, as grey clouds steal in from the west, the finest drizzle settles like forgiveness on the landscape.

A pair of oak-trees cast a broad shadow over us as we trundle past. And then we enter into the silence of a wood of elder and alder, ash and chestnut, crab apple and copper beech – and towering above them all, giant poplars and sycamores...

And along the banks of the canal grows a profusion of giant hogweed, dog rose, wild honeysuckle, meadowsweet and marsh marigolds...

We pass a large field on which a thousand clever crows are going about their business, earning their living in the way that crows do: scratching, listening with their heads cocked, snapping up a titbit.

We follow a sharp turn in the canal and an invisible billow of perfume envelopes me. It's the broom, in extravagant bloom.

And when we moor for the night in some solitary spot, it's to the tune of birdsong. A solitary blackbird takes up a position in the hawthorn on our flank and serenades us in melody that seems never to repeat itself.

All this washes over me: a constantly changing panoply of natural things. There's not a thought in my head: it's all sensation.

And when something shakes me out of this waking reverie, I

feel… full. As if the hunger I'd experienced has been more than satisfied – by this rich diet of colour and smell, sound and the perfectly tactile experience of sun and drizzle, wind and rain.

And I think, surely this not only feeds my imagination, but also triggers the creative impulse?

Just a thought.

(Or maybe simply a sensation.)

AT THE HEART OF STORY, A WRETCHED CONUNDRUM

Paul Smith was an entrepreneur who devoted 80 hours a week to keeping his business afloat. (That is, as you will see, an apt metaphor.) The work was so demanding, and the Great Recession so crippling, that he found himself managing a bankrupt business, and presiding over a dysfunctional marriage.

Trish had followed his story on the blog he wrote – and as we approached Wigrams Turn, where the South Oxford Canal meets the Grand Union, she called out:

"Look, there's the marina where Paul Smith lives."

She told me about him as we chugged down the Oxford Canal into the serene surroundings of north Oxfordshire.

"What happened then?" I asked.

"Well, when things fell apart, he looked for outdoor work. He thought he could do with a change from the pressure of business life. He landed a job at Calcutt Boats, as a groundsman."

That was Calcutt's Boats, which we'd just passed.

Paul, Trish told me, bought a venerable and clapped-out narrowboat called James, and despite the fact that he had no resources and no partner to shoulder the burdens of failure, slowly he started to put his life together once again.

Tracy Todd had everything going for her. A husband she adored. A baby she would have given her life for. A vital, energetic and beautiful woman, she lived with her family on an idyllic farm not far from the Kruger Park in South Africa.

And then, on the long road back from a family holiday in 1998, their baby son, Chad, cocooned in his car seat in the back, started niggling. Tracy loosened her seatbelt to attend to him. At that moment, the car ahead of them had a blowout. Tracy's husband took evasive action, swung to the left, and lost control.

The car tumbled off the road into a field and came to rest on its roof. Tracy came down hard on her head. She knew at once that something bad had happened – but her first thought, of course, was for Chad.

He was fine, as it happened.

But Tracy had broken her neck, and she found herself a quadriplegic, paralysed from the neck down, permanently relegated to life in a wheelchair. Her husband abandoned her, taking custody of her son. She was driven to the very verge of suicide.

Tracy, though, fought back. She was determined to prove to the world, but more importantly, to herself, that she was capable of leading an independent life and that she would, despite having lost custody, raise her son.

Then, take an old school friend of mine. He went to the best schools. He scored an accountancy degree at university. He landed a series of good jobs, ending as financial director of a large media company. He married well, but late, fathering a couple of children. He enjoyed life to the full. His passion was hunting.

It was on the return flight from a hunting trip that the private plane which he and a group of friends had chartered, and flown by an experienced pilot, unaccountably went down a few hundred metres from the runaway and all on board were killed.

~

These are all real stories. If they were dramatised in print, which ones would we really want to read? Which, do you imagine, would grab us by the throats and engage us on a deeply emotional level?

I'd say that nine out of ten – no, ninety nine out of a hundred – readers will instantly recognise that the story of a man who faced no obstacles, whose path was bestrewn with connections and good fortune, is not really a story at all, however tragic his end.

His would be the life we wanted to live, perhaps – but not the story we wanted to read.

Stories concern the problems that people face and, more importantly, the ways in which they solve them.

How did Paul Smith turn his life around? How did he recover from the twin blows of losing his wife and his business? His journey is one that we would want to read about, is my guess.

And to an even greater degree, Tracy's story of her return to a full and vigorous life, despite not having control over much more than the finger of one hand, is a hugely engaging one. How she wrestled circumstance into yielding a life full of love and accomplishment is an account that will leave no reader unmoved.

Never forget, at the heart of every great story lies a wretched conundrum, apparently insoluble, that your hero has to grapple with.

Paul's story unrolled on a continuous basis on a blog he wrote for many years about his life on a narrowboat, the adventures it afforded him, and the challenges he met.

Tracy's story is told vividly and with powerful restraint in the book she wrote called *Brave Lotus Flower Rides the Dragon.* It was an instant best seller when it was published in South Africa some years ago. It remains available through Amazon.

We were privileged to be able to work with her on the manuscript.

Good stories are about difficulties overcome, and the lessons we can learn from them. The greater the difficulty, the more compelling the story.

OF COURSE, GIN HELPS

In Oxford, we moored at the visitors' moorings in Jericho, yards from a pedestrian bridge that led into the warren of streets of the old canal warehouse section of the city – and, we soon discovered, a revered pub called The Old Bookbinders Ale House where, on Fridays, a giant tub of mussels was available for just ten quid.

More important even than the mussels, was the fact that the Oxford Literary Festival was in full swing. It featured, as always, a stellar cast of celebrity writers including, on that occasion, Philip Pullman, scheduled to have a conversation with the Sunday Times children's books editor, Nicolette Jones at the Sheldonian Theatre. The event celebrated the twentieth anniversary of his acclaimed trilogy, for children, *His Dark Materials.*

I'd devoured the trilogy some years before, and was dazzled by its invention, its daring and its sheer ambition. As Nicky Henderson, a writer in the student newspaper Cherwell, wrote at about the same time: "... *His Dark Materials*, (is) a trilogy aimed at children, (but it) covers broken families, betrayal, war, loss of the soul, death, the afterlife, sexual discovery, unrequited love, and even the end of God."

We were lucky to secure two of the last available tickets.

During the course of his conversation with Nicolette, Pullman was quizzed by a number of his young readers. One boy, no older than fourteen or so, put a very pertinent, writerly question to the acclaimed author.

"Have your stories," he asked, "ever dried up?"

You could hear a hum of adult amusement sweep through the Sheldonian Theatre. But Pullman quite rightly took the question entirely seriously.

"Yes," he said. "But as a professional writer, you've just got to push on." He paused a moment, then added: "Of course, gin helps."

Then he described his writing routine. He sets himself a target every day of three pages. Once he achieves that goal, he stops, even though he might feel eager to continue.

"And if I'm having difficulty writing, I *force* myself to go on writing until I've done those three pages."

It's good, he explained, to stop when you're going well, because it's easy then to pick up when you start again the next day.

"And if it's going badly, then my rule forces me to continue," he said.

Which reminded me of a similar rule that Anthony Trollope observed. Until he retired, he worked for the Post Office in Ireland and later England as a surveyor's clerk. When he was not on the road visiting far-flung corners of the kingdom, he set aside two hours a day for his writing – from five in the morning till seven. He made it a rule to stop writing the very moment the small hand hit seven and the big one twelve, even if he was in the middle of one of those complex Victorian sentences.

I'm not sure if he said as much, or if I inferred the reasoning behind this habit, but it seems to me clear that if you do this – stop in the midst of a rolling sentence – then you have an automatic head start the next time you take up your pen – or turn on your laptop.

I don't suffer from writers' block myself, and never have,

probably because much of my writing has been done in response to a commission – and you don't eat if you don't meet your deadlines.

But this seems to me as good a prophylactic against the dreaded block as any I've come across.

LOSING YOUR READER'S TRUST

We planned to spend a couple of weeks in Oxford before taking to the Thames for an exploratory trip upstream to the limits of the river's navigation at Lechlade.

There was plenty of action at the Literary Festival to keep us absorbed however. But before I moved on to other writers, I gleaned another important insight from Philip Pullman.

Remember that *His Dark Materials,* and, more recently, the second trilogy, *The Book of Dust*, featuring the same central character, Lyra Belacqua, are only the more recent of his books. Long before he began work on *Northern Lights,* the first book in the sequence, he'd written a series of thrillers, also for children, set in Victorian London, featuring the feisty Sally Lockhart.

"They were all melodramas," he told his audience in Oxford's Sheldonian Theatre, "but I took great care to get the Victorian backdrop as accurate as I could."

For instance, he found Ordinance Survey maps of London from the 1870s, and used these to plot the movement of his characters.

"I found out what cab rides cost from, say, Piccadilly to Blackfriars."

He researched the rapidly growing science of photography, since he wished to use it as the subject of one of the Sally Lockhart mysteries.

But why go to all this trouble? Who would ever know what a cab from one point of 1870 London to another would have cost? Would anyone ever challenge him if he happened to get a detail wrong? Do details like this matter – or are they only the concerns of an obsessive?

Well, of course it matters. How dare you suggest otherwise. And here's why:

Any given fiction is a lie. We all know this. We realise that the characters who feature in novels don't and never did exist. We know that the action described never happened. And yet we are prepared to suspend our disbelief in the world the writer has created because we wish to be entertained... taken out of ourselves... magicked into the larger realms of the imagination...

And the more fantastical that world, the more tenuous its relation is to any world we've encountered, the more vital it is that we maintain the illusion of reality. And how do we do that? By making as much of our fictional world as possible as real as possible, by building it on well-researched foundations, by using details that our readers recognise from the world they know...

These factors relate to the reader. But it's also true that the writer feels more confident if he's proceeding on the basis of ascertained facts.

So, if, like Pullman, you wish to write a fantasy of some description, then there is no better advice than that you undertake the most thoroughgoing research programme before you begin. In order to get the details right. In order to make those backdrops as convincing as possible. In order to persuade your reader willingly to swallow the bigger lie of your impossible story which might involve giants, or extra-terrestrial aliens, or telepathy or, more simply, that rarest of all phenomena, an honest politician.

Another writer in a different forum – Joanne Harris, of

Chocolat fame – told us that "you can lie, but you can't cheat". And I think that's precisely what Pullman was saying:

Stories are lies. Of course they are. But you can't cheat your reader by lying about the cost of a cab from Piccadilly to Blackfriars, however unlikely it is they'll ever check. You can't cheat your reader by inventing procedures a real police force would never use. You can't cheat your readers by relying on guesses when only hard facts will do.

It's difficult enough to persuade readers that the world you've created is not just a possible version of reality, but a probable one. And awfully easy to lose their trust. A book a friend read a while ago described the view that the protagonist obtained driving from O.R. Tambo Airport into Johannesburg – and put the iconic tower of the Carlton Centre in the wrong place.

It profoundly affected her enjoyment of the book. As she said, "if you can't trust your author to get the *factual* details right, how can you follow them on their *fictional* journey?"

So, this injunction to research and check the facts that underpin your story is addressed not only to writers of fantasy. Every book, however mundane, creates a world in which the action of the story plays out.

We are, in other words, all world-builders – and we need to take our responsibilities seriously.

RESEARCH COMES IN TWO FLAVOURS

The kind of research that writers do before they begin writing their novels comes in two flavours.

On the bottom shelf, in the pale pink bottle, there's the sort of research you do in order to get the elements of your story right.

You're writing a police procedural? Well, then, for goodness sake find out what the relevant police procedure is.

Writing a medical thriller involving illegal organ harvesting? Then attend a kidney transplant to get the pictures of the surgery firmly fixed in your mind. (And if every surgeon in the country turns down your requests to attend such an operation, then look online until you find what you're after. It's all there, believe me!)

But there's a different kind of research. It comes in the emerald green bottle on one of the upper shelves. It's not the solution to a problem – but the inspiration for story.

At the Oxford Literary Festival, the thriller writer Christopher Fowler, author of a celebrated series of oddball whodunnits featuring two detectives called Bryant and May, talked about a novel he was writing set in London during the Blitz. He'd read all the usual books on conditions in the city at the time, he'd watched documentaries, he'd done his homework.

And none of it really did the trick. He needed the sorts of details that ordinary histories don't provide.

But then he remembered that his mother had herself lived through the Blitz.

"She'd worked," he said, "as a legal secretary in The Strand." He wondered what she remembered about the period.

"Oh," she said, "I remember the telephone directories."

"The telephone directories? What telephone directories?" He hoped her mind wasn't beginning to deteriorate.

"Well," she said, acerbic in the face of his doubt, "when shop windows were blown out, they filled them with sandbags – but when they ran out of sandbags, they stuffed old telephone directories into the gaps where windows had been. Used directories."

Now that, Fowler said, is not something that you'd ever find in regular histories of the time, or online. It's a detail that could only have been reported by someone who'd been on the spot. And it was a detail that, he said, he used to great good effect in his novel.

So, when you need the sort of textural detail that simply brings a story alive, don't rely only on the "official" history – seek out someone who was there (if that's possible), and ask them what they remember, what struck them with particular force about the event they witnessed.

This goes for more than specific incidents. You're writing a story that involves a horrific motorcar accident? Well, then, go talk to a tow truck driver, or a paramedic, who's attended more horrific motorcar accidents than you've had hot dinners. Ask him to tell you about what he looks for when he arrives at the scene of an accident. Ask him for details of the sorts of things that he's seen thrown clear of the colliding motorcars. Ask him what he most fears as he's racing to the scene, and what he most hopes for.

And then allow these impressions to guide you as you develop story around the fictional accident in your novel.

~

After our Oxford sojourn, we were ready to move on. Our map suggested that the exit from the canal, the Isis Lock Junction, lay just three quarters of a furlong beyond our mooring. Yes, canal maps still measure distances shorter than a mile in furlongs.

Beyond that, well, the Thames for us was a slightly intimidating prospect. It stretches for 135 miles from Lechlade to the sea through forty-five locks. It's a river, of course, which puts it in a very different category from that of canals, where the water hardly moves. It's deep, where canals are generally no deeper than four feet or so. And it's home to a whole different population of boats, ranging from giant steamers to single-handed university sculls.

Apart from the inherent challenges of river navigation, we'd also been worried by the incessant rain that had been falling. The catchment area of the Thames is vast, encompassing most of the Cotswolds and beyond. We'd been keeping a close eye on the relevant websites which contained warnings of flooding on the river.

We'd learned that when the river authorities mounted Red Boards at locks, it meant that cruising was dangerous. Yellow Boards were cautionary in effect: you could navigate but had to beware strong currents.

Red Boards were up at every lock on the Thames.

So we waited, checking the Environment Agency every day.

Finally, several days after our scheduled departure, the Red Boards were down, and Yellow Boards were up.

Now, we were planning a leisurely two-week cruise down the Thames, getting to London a day or two before the start of the Olympics. If we waited for the Yellow Boards to come down, we might put that schedule in jeopardy.

"So let's go," I urged.

"Will one more day make much difference?" Trish can be – but isn't always – more cautious that I am.

"Probably not. Tomorrow morning, then."

And so, the next day, at eight or so, I was at my place at the tiller, Trish on the canal path.

"Ready to cast off?" It makes more sense for me to steer Patience, while Trish casts off, ties up and operates the locks (which can be a tricky business, which we'll get to later) – but the truth is, she regards the business of steering our boat with some trepidation.

"It's because you have to move the tiller to the right, to steer left. It seems unnatural."

Now she pushed the prow off the bank, leapt on board at the last moment, and we were off.

2

SECOND VOYAGE

THE THAMES

THE GRANDEST TRADITION OF THEM ALL

Once you're through the final – or first – lock on the Oxford Canal, Isis Lock, you have to duck under a couple of railway bridges before the canal meets the river. One of these is so low that Patience barely squeezed under it.

And then we turned left, or to use the expression that we nautical types prefer, we altered course to port.

And almost immediately the alarm bells went off in my mind.

The river was running fast.

"Perhaps you're not used to rivers," Trish said. She'd joined me on the deck.

We were whizzing along at some speed. A narrowboat weighs upwards of ten tons. Our four stroke Nanni drove us along canals at a stately – or more accurately, a geriatric – two to three miles an hour.

Clearly, on the Thames, we were travelling at twice that speed at least.

"I thought Yellow Boards meant it was safe?" I said, narrowly avoiding a gin palace plastic cruiser moored up at Osney Island, which is not an island at all, but a very desirable patch of real estate, liable, however, to flooding.

"Perhaps you've got your foot on the accelerator," Trish said.

Well, she was wrong on two counts. The throttle is hand-held, and far from having my foot – or hand – down, I had throttled back as far as I could without turning the engine off completely.

"There's the lock already," Trish said. She was right. Osney Lock lay a couple of hundred metres ahead. To the right of us, water gushed in great arcs through the gaps of a sluice.

"I'm going to hit the landing stage hard," I warned.

Seconds later I did indeed hit the landing stage, just above the lock, very hard, nearly knocking Trish off her feet, and me off my navigation chair, and put the engine into hard reverse.

A moment later we'd stopped, without, remarkably, hitting the lock gates. Trish lashed us to the bollards on the floating landing.

Firmly attached to the lock gates was a large notice, warning craft not to proceed. It wasn't just a red board, it was a Red Board.

A minute later, the lock-keeper sauntered out of the lock buildings. "Red Boards are up," he said, mildly.

"They weren't this morning," I responded, a little defensively. "At least, not on your website."

"No," he conceded. "But the river rose sharply this morning."

"How long will it take to go down?"

He shrugged laconically. "Difficult to say. A few days... A few weeks. It all depends."

So, as I write this, Patience is moored up at Osney Lock. It's raining again. We're unable to move down – or upstream until the Red Boards come down, and that won't happen until the rain, feeding the Thames with indigestible quantities of water, ceases.

But Oxford, we'd already discovered, is a grand place to be marooned in. And one of the chief reasons is the existence of the city's newly refurbished Ashmolean Museum, full of curiosities, antiquities and a small but perfect collection of Pre-Raphaelite art.

But our lesson, today, is drawn from a smallish room in the basement of the museum devoted to Reading and Writing. Some of the very earliest examples of writing are on display, from Sumeria and Mesopotamia four and five thousand years ago.

And while I was studying ancient tablets inscribed with extraordinarily well-preserved examples of Linear A and Linear B – among the very first scripts devised by humankind and used to record harvests of wheat, and livestock numbers – this thought occurred to me:

The cleverest of our ancestors invented writing. The cleverest of their descendants realised it was possible to use squiggles on papyrus and, later, vellum and, later still, paper, to record not only what land they owned, or what transactions they entered into, or the size of their crops but also their stories...

Gilgamesh was the first great saga, followed by the Greek epics and tragedies.

Religions waded in with their own stories.

Cervantes recorded the "history" of Don Quixote's adventures. Shakespeare, Ben Jonson, Middleton, Marlowe...

By the 18th and 19th centuries, the trickle had become, like the Thames, a flood of great and lasting literature.

And today we, the heirs of this truly extraordinary intellectual tradition of writing and reading, one of the jewels, perhaps *the* jewel in humanity's crown, use it to sell breakfast cereal; write incomprehensible instructions for electronic gadgets or flatpack furniture assembly; compose the most trivial of television programmes...

And yet it remains possible for each of us to recapture some of the original magic of writing. Every time we lift a pen, or fire up our laptops, we declare ourselves the true heirs of those Mesopotamian farmers, capable of inscribing something lasting, something that *our* descendants might one day celebrate.

WHEN A LOCK BECOMES THE KEY

We were marooned at Osney Lock for six days. I fretted for the first day or two.

"We'll be late for the Olympics," I said.

"No, we won't," Trish said. "We'll just have to go a little faster down the Thames, that's all."

She was, of course, right. There's no arguing with the weather, or with Red Boards. So, you might as well relax and enjoy your enforced idleness.

When, eventually, the lock-keeper announced that we were free to go, we had just five days left before the Olympics kicked off.

We set off at, well, not high speed, of course, given both the limits of narrowboats, but also the speed limits on river traffic. On canals, the limit is four mph; on rivers, eight. And although, unassisted we weren't able to go much faster than five; we had the river itself to help us along.

At something close to eight mph, we scampered down the Thames. Most of the locks are manned, which helped. All much bigger than any locks on the canal system, which meant that we usually had to share them with other boats – sometimes large passenger-carrying river boats; sometimes small flotillas of canoes and kayaks.

We arrived at Teddington Lock four days after leaving Oxford. It's the largest of all the locks on the Thames – in fact there are two locks, one much larger than the other. Beyond it lies the tidal Thames; before it the relatively tame weir-ed and locked reach of the river.

Teddington is very firmly under the control of the lock keeping authorities. You're allowed through only at high tide. In the hour or so before that, all the boats whose skippers have booked passage, are ushered into the lock.

We squeezed in between a broad-beam and a river steamer. Ahead of us was a host of other boats of every possible description: skiffs, rowing boats, narrowboats both long and short, a Dutch barge or two and who knows what else.

We expected the water level in the lock to drop us down to the level of the tidal Thames. But nothing much happened.

And then suddenly, we were all moving on, and we realised that at high tide there is hardly any difference in level between the tidal and the non-tidal rivers.

The tidal Thames, we soon learned, is a writhing, contained beast of a river whose coils you can feel flexing beneath the surface of the water. We passed by the iconic riverine islands, Eel Pie Island and Monkey Island Estate among them, and then, opposite Kew Gardens, described a wide arc and entered the Grand Union Canal at Brentford, in London's far west. It'd still take us five hours or more to get to our destination, Paddington Basin, just off Little Venice.

One of the first challenges to greet you at the London end of the Grand Union is a flight of locks, the Hanwell Locks, that run up alongside a Victorian asylum for the insane. The walls of the asylum are handsome and high. If you listen very carefully, you can just hear the faintest echoes of the gloom and the chaos that must once have ruled there.

Now the Hanwell Locks, six in number, are remarkable in two respects. Firstly, they are unusually deep. Secondly, they are not in good nick. Their gates are splintered, the gear that opens their sluices in bad need of refurbishment. And they leak. Badly.

You might not know how a lock works.

When you're ascending a flight – as we are, from sea level at the Thames – you approach a lock from below. Let's assume that the lock behind the closed gates is full of water. On the canals, where nearly all the locks are unmanned, your first task is to empty the lock. This you do by opening small sluice gates set in the gates themselves – in the wide locks of the Grand Union, there are two gates at either end. The water rushes out until the level of water in the lock equals the level of water in the canal below the lock. You open the gates, steer your canal boat into the lock, and close the gates behind it.

Then it's simply a matter of opening the sluices in the upper gates which raises the water in the lock – and the boat floating in it – until it reaches the level of the canal above the lock. Finally, you open the upper gates and chug out.

If the water in the lock is even a half inch lower than the water in the canal above it, it will prove impossible to open the gates thanks to the pressure of water holding them shut.

So, the scene is set. Trish has opened the gates to the first lock of the Hanwell flight. I have steered Patience into the lock. She has closed the gates and opened the sluices in the upper gate. Water has gushed in, raising Patience and me some ten feet. Now she prepares to open the top gates. First, she closes the sluices on one gate, and crosses over to the other. Then she pushes at the great arm of the gate. It's delicately balanced on a pivot so that, although it weighs upwards of a ton, it's usually fairly easy to manipulate.

But not this time. This time the gate resists all her efforts to open it. Why?

She opens the sluices again. We hear the gates click subtly as the water levels in and out of the lock equalise. She closes the sluices, crosses swiftly to the other gate and tries to push it open. No go.

She repeats this process three times. All in vain. She realises that water is leaking out of the lock so fast that she has to leave the sluices open while she opens the gate. This, note, is not usual procedure. It is more laborious and it takes more time. Because in the time it took her to close the sluices of one gate, and cross to the other gate, the water level in the lock has dropped fractionally below the level of water in the canal above. And why is that? Because the lower gates are leaking prodigiously.

Now what, you might ask, has this to do with writing? And my answer is simple: a lot. How often do we find that something in a scene we're writing doesn't work? It feels flat. There's no sense of drama. The character is a marionette without any internal life.

In short, our story is leaking. In order to fix it we have to pause and take stock. What precisely is the problem? Is it that your protagonist's decision is unmotivated? Is it that you've left out an essential set-up scene which means that your readers are likely to be confused? Is it that a character is just slightly off? Perhaps the conflict is not quite well defined enough – or we're working towards a dramatic destination that shifts even as we work our way through the scene.

There could, of course, be any one of a great many problems.

But there *is* point in urging you to pause, take a good hard look at the scene, identify the problem, and rectify it. Sometimes it is very difficult to sort out what the problem really is. Sometimes it takes trial and error. It can entail rewriting a scene or two, even a chapter or two. On occasion it might even entail starting at the beginning again. This could take time. It could entail your trying a number of different solutions before finding the one that really works. It means being patient. It means waiting for the water level in the lock to equalise with the water level in the pound above. Before the story and the characters click into place.

Only then will you be ready to steam on with your story.

You might be asking how we ever managed to steam out of that lock? Well, Trish located the cause of the problem. It wasn't a plot problem or a character problem; it wasn't a question of motivation.

It was a branch caught in the hinge of the lower gate. It took just a minute to yank it out. The lock then filled beautifully, the top gates opened smoothly, and we were out and away.

LESSONS FROM THE OLYMPICS

Two centuries ago, Paddington Basin was the terminus of the Paddington Canal, that led from the Grand Junction Canal into the heart of London.

It was a hive of commercial activity, surrounded by wharves and warehouses through which a steady stream of bricks, clay, coal, hay, cattle and vegetables moved.

The basin had been opened to great public rejoicing twenty years before. Flags fluttered in the breeze, peals of bells rang out over the city, and spectators were thrilled by the boom of cannons.

We were lucky to find a mooring in the basin at all. To begin with, we were moored up against another boat – it's called breasting up in boating jargon – but the next day a berth became available, and we moved in snugly against the quay, just spitting distance from a handy restaurant.

Having made the trip down the Thames in just four days, the plan had been to make our way to the spanking new Olympic Park for at least a glimpse of the Games. But we were sick. First Trish and then I went down with a bad case of flu, and, miserably, we battened down the hatches and prepared to wait it out.

However, we *had* invested in a little 12-volt television monitor, so we were able to keep half a bleary eye on events a dozen miles to the east in Hackney Wick.

But before we get to the actual Games, let's consider what lessons they might offer writers both of fiction and non-fiction.

Let me go back to one of the great story templates. Anyone involved in the writing of fiction will, surely, have heard of Joseph Campbell and his great Hero's Journey thesis? Let me refresh your memory, briefly:

The hero (of any myth, legend, novel or movie – and for "hero" also read "heroine") starts in the familiar realm of the everyday world. With elegance in mind, let me assume for the moment that our hero is a heroine. She is challenged to action by an inciting incident, to leave the familiar world on a quest that will necessarily take her into unfamiliar territory – a strange world filled with unknown antagonists.

She will have to meet various challenges and undergo a number of trials or tests. In due course she will find her way to the citadel where her nemesis hangs out, and will there engage in battle with the enemy, dying in the process.

Reborn, the heroine makes her way back to the familiar world with some deep insight, what Campbell called a "boon" which she will share with her friends or community.

That (in a very small nutshell) is the Hero's Journey, pared down to its bare bones.

It is an extraordinarily powerful template which underpins, Joseph Campbell says, all the myths, legends and fairytales ever told – and, arguably, all the stories we've ever told each other in any form, whether as novel, movie, or the most casual of bedtime stories told by a distracted mother to an entranced child.

Now let's look at your typical Olympic event...

For every contestant, the trip to London represents the journey into the unfamiliar world. When they get there, they meet a number of assailants as their skills and their strength and their endurance are tested across a range of preliminary events in order to qualify for the right to challenge the very best in the world in the finals of their discipline.

That challenge is Campbell's assault on the citadel, the attempt to overthrow the old order. If they triumph and emerge from that test with a medal, their old selves – as neophytes with hope in their hearts and determination of steel – die, and they emerge as the new generation of world beaters, able to return to their own countries with tales of their derring-do, and a thousand lessons to pass on to the next flight of hopefuls – not to mention bags of money from eager sponsors.

In other words, dear writers, the trajectory of an Olympic athlete fighting to beat the best in London is identical to the trajectory of the story you wish to tell of a heroine overcoming the odds in her fight to find and embrace true love.

Your heroine undergoes trials as ingenious as any you can devise which test her resolve, her steadiness of purpose and her moral fibre. She meets her nemesis – a rival, or someone who, not to put too fine a point on it, does not have her best interests at heart – proves her love for the hero, and emerges victorious with him ready to impart her new understanding of romantic love to the world.

Although Trish and I were very far from being Olympians, we had undergone our own tests and trials on our way down the Thames: a flood to start with, a mad dash to get to London on time and a desperate struggle up the Hanwell flight of locks. Then, we endured our dark night of the soul doing battle with the dreaded flu lurgy in Paddington Basin.

But finally we emerged, reborn to health and vitality, ready for the next challenge: the passage along the Regent's Canal to Limehouse Basin in the east.

But before I tell you of that journey, let's ponder a few more reflections that watching the Olympics on our little screen engendered in me. Read on!

STORIES ARE MEMORABLE, SPECTACLE NOT SO MUCH

I'm not sure what you remember of the grand opening ceremony of the London 2012 Olympic Games? Sniffling and coughing, we watched the opening on our television screen until the wee hours of Saturday morning.

Although we both enjoyed it immensely, I couldn't help analysing it in story and dramatic terms.

Let's begin by comparing it to the Beijing opening ceremony of 2008. Remember that? It was spectacular, no doubt about that. No one can deny that Beijing offered spectacle of an unforgettable kind. I remember so well the massed drummers working in perfect synchrony... The massed... Mmm. I can't seem to remember what else happened. Massed... *something*... Swordsmen? Archers? I remember that cute singer who really impressed us all until we discovered that she'd been chosen for her cuteness, and that, actually, it was some other less cute little girl who'd sung the lyrics...

I do remember that everything was extraordinarily impressive. But I have to confess that I don't remember that much of the content. Lights. Fireworks. Conjured out of the latest technology and an ancient mastery of pyrotechnics. Loads and loads of synchronised *stuff*.

The British opening ceremony was not nearly as visually stunning – although it certainly had its moments.

But I'm betting that in four years time I'll remember far more of this narrative than I remember of Beijing's. Why?

Because there *was* a narrative. A story that drove the spectacle forward. The opening sequence featured the bucolic past. A kind of prelapsarian paradise featuring an idealised countryside filled with happy farmers, village greens, and the iconic thwack of willow on leather.

This all comes to an end when the infernal engines of the industrial revolution launch Britain's age of steam. Chimneys rise across the land. Armies of industrial workers emerge from the new factories that spread, like a plague, across England's green and pleasant land.

Industrialisation was both a curse – and the foundation of the nation's prosperity.

Out of the chaos rises a new fight for justice – by the workers on the one hand, by women on the other.

One of the victories of this struggle is the establishment of a health service for all...

And so on. There's one grand over-arching story, with other shorter stories wrapped up within this.

There is a narrative logic to the spectacle – a logic that sticks in the mind. A logic of cause and effect, of set-up and pay-off, of act and consequence, that binds us to the unfolding story.

In Beijing, however impressive the massed drummers were, there was no story.

And of course, it is precisely the logic of story that needs to inform our writing. Sheer spectacle, while impressive, doesn't really cut it, does it?

When we devise story, we need to look for the connections, the sinews that hold our brilliant scenes together, the motivation that drives characters to make, and then regret their decisions, the emotional logic that reveals how a coward can become a hero; a housewife, an adventurer; a Mafia boss, a victim of his own bad decisions.

While we slowly recover from flu, venturing out for a steak roll and a glass of wine at the restaurant on our doorstep, or taking a short walk to the roll-up bridge that is a feature of the basin, we plan our next move.

London, we've already learned, is crammed full of narrowboats filled with liveaboards. Boats are a much more affordable option than even the cheapest land-bound accommodation. Yes, we found a berth in Paddington Basin with comparative ease, but along the Regent's Canal we have little doubt we will struggle to find one.

But in Limehouse Basin there is a berth reserved for disabled boaters.

This is rare on the waterways, and perhaps it will be in great demand, but it is a distinct possibility.

But Limehouse will have to wait – we have one more Olympic tale to tell.

FLAWED CHAMPIONS

The night before we left Paddington Basin, we watched the extraordinary closing ceremony of the Paralympics, and I was struck by a thought – the last to be inspired by that summer of sport, I promise you! – about the stories that rattle about us in every possible direction.

This was my thought: Every athlete in the Olympics, obviously, has a story to tell – of promise, opportunities taken, hard work, victory, defeat and triumph. Every athlete's on a hero's journey. Every race, every contest, is a hero's journey.

This is all a given, a pedestrian truth of competitive athletics.

But the *Paralympians*, these flawed champions, are in another category entirely.

An image springs to mind of a young woman, hair bound tightly beneath a scarf, clearly suffering from very severe cerebral palsy, in a wheelchair with a shot in her hand, preparing to heave it. Her head weaves from side to side, in the coils of the cerebral accident that has her in its thrall. But her eyes are bright and focused with ambition, and, for a second, the cerebral palsy relaxes its hold on her and her arm shoots forward, the shot describes a neat parabola and lands on the turf just a few metres from her.

And I think: who is this woman, what is her story, how can

one explain that burning ambition in a body so broken by circumstance?

And, however meagre the outcome, how sweet, how deep the sense of accomplishment!

Another image: the South African Fanie van der Merwe, who snatched gold in the final centimetres of his 100-metre race when he threw himself at the tape with such disregard, with such recklessness that he stumbled and fell immediately he'd breached it. But the gold was safely in his grasp, the dream he'd dreamt now a reality.

And finally, there's the story – or whole suite of stories – of the swimmers competing in the 800 metres final.

The best of these swimmers were very good, faster than most able-bodied swimmers, sleek as seals in the water. As the winner ploughed to the finish line, the watching crowd rose to their feet, cheering his victory.

Second and third duly received similar accolades. In fact, as each of the swimmers ended the race, the crowd accorded them cheers of acknowledgement.

But their most especial ovation was reserved for the swimmer who came in last, a full length and a half behind the swimmer immediately before him.

For that length and a half, he was the only swimmer still in action, slowly windmilling his way towards his goal. And by the time he got there, the crowd was not only on its feet – they were roaring fit to bust.

It was the richness of these stories that for me made the Paralympics the more rewarding spectacle.

And it reminded me, if I needed reminding, that the world is, in fact, no more than a vast warehouse stuffed full of stories.

And it's our task, and our duty, and our privilege to tell them.

THE DEVIL'S IN THE DETAIL

It takes a day to cross London on the Regent's Canal from Paddington Basin in the heart of the West End to Limehouse Basin in the east. It's a journey of nine miles and descends through twelve locks. It took us all of seven and a half hours through a rare day of August sun.

It's difficult to describe the extraordinary variety of sights and scenes, of people active on the tow path and in cafes and restaurants along the way, of wildlife on the canal, of aircraft constantly heading in to and out of at least three airports, of enormous building sites along the way, but it provides an instant lesson for writers intent on capturing a mood – or capturing a city – in words.

You could try by using words like "magnificent," "great," "extraordinary," "boundless," "astonishing," "bewildering" and so on and so forth. These would constitute an attempt to explain the impact on us of London, viewed from our narrowboat. It's true: we remarked repeatedly on the vibrancy of the city, on the life of the canal path, on the energy of the people...

You could try to do it in this way, but you'd fail – because all of those words, and many hundreds of other similar ones – are simply too vague, too generic, to capture the unique essence of the city.

The only way you can do it is by descending the ladder of generality into the cellar of the very specific and particular. By observing and describing the details. Here are just three examples drawn from today's odyssey:

I'll begin with an altercation. The antagonists are two coots, sooty grey water birds featuring a distinctive white beak and a blaze of white above it. They're having a fierce and noisy fight, their wings half-raised aggressively, their feet up, their claws seeking an advantage. And they're squawking with uninhibited abandon.

Their battle takes place in a section of the canal that is green with duck weed – so solid a carpet that you wouldn't be surprised to see someone confidently striding across the canal on it. But as the coots have at each other, they plough through the duckweed, creating channels of black through the green.

And then suddenly one of the coots calls it quits and turns and dashes away. The victorious coot races after him, his head held low above the water in a particularly threatening way. A third coot then enters the scene: it's a fledgling and it's crying piteously. Both of the adults, intent on chasing and escaping, ignore it.

And by then we've moved on and I miss the final outcome of the affray...*

~

Joggers hammer past us in an uneven stream. One in particular, a woman, has all the gear you could imagine, including a black heart monitor velcroed round her upper arm. She's ripped: her quads, her biceps, her triceps rippling as she runs, and her blonde pony-tail, threaded through a fashionable cap, swishes rhythmically from side to side.

Briefly we keep pace with her – but then she draws ahead and disappears round the next turn of the canal.

We pass through the locks at Camden Market. Large crowds of onlookers observe Trish as she fills the lock, swings the lock gates to, and opens the paddles.

Narrowboaters call these spectators gongoozlers. In our experience, gongoozlers are capable of standing within feet of us, watching us curiously and without any visible self-consciousness, as we perform the most pedestrian of routines – throwing a rope over a bollard, using our bargepole to fend off a floating log, pouring a cup of tea while we wait for a lock to fill.

We have some idea of what a chimpanzee might feel being observed by visitors to the zoo.

Later, at Commercial Road Lock – the lock that opens into Limehouse Basin itself – we're confronted by a group of youngsters, some teens, some in their early twenties, swinging on the lock gate. A couple of them fool around with a litre bottle of Coke, throwing it half in fun, half with an edge of aggression, at each other. One of the young men has a shaven head and wears a tight t-shirt over impressive musculature. He features a great many tattoos, the most distinctive one of which is a colourful Chinese dragon.

All in all, the young men are vaguely intimidating – although, when we ask them to stand aside and let us operate the gate, they fall back passively, without argument and watch, unsmiling, as we descend through the lock.

What works here is not talk of a vibrant, even a great city. What works are the details – the very specific details – that the writer observes and recalls. Observe and recall this advice the next time you sit down to write a scene.

. . .

* Much later, moored on a lake on the outskirts of Bedford, we learned that these seasonal battles between coots – the oldest story of all: males fighting for the favours of females – not infrequently end in the untimely death of one of the combatants. Coots play for very high stakes indeed.

THERE AND BACK AGAIN

We've been cruising the canals now for some years. Our favourite cruise is a circular one. From A to B, but then not simply back to A in time to catch our flight back to South Africa, but back to A via C.

The canal system abounds in opportunities: the Warwickshire Ring, the Four Counties Ring. Our largest circular expedition – hardly circular, but you get what I mean – was from Braunston to Manchester then, via the Leeds and Liverpool Canal, over the Pennines to Leeds. From Leeds we took a series of canals that led down to the River Trent, then meandered upstream towards Nottingham (taking a detour into Lincoln and back along a canal originally excavated by the Romans) before finally mooring up where we began, in Braunston.

But it's not always possible to avoid the linear A to B and B to A.

From Limehouse Basin, we proposed cruising up the Lee – or Lea – to Bishop's Stortford. That's as far as you can go in a narrowboat, and so, perforce you have to turn tail and return along the route back to Limehouse.

It's not a giant leap from these thoughts to this:

One of my favourite definitions of art is that it is repetition with variation. There are, we all sadly acknowledge, no new ideas in the world – just old ones presented in new ways. There is, after all, no getting away from the fact that there are a finite number of plots knocking around.

These observations – old ones, often recycled, as they must be by the logic of my own argument - recurred on our trip out of London and up the River Lee. It is not always the most beautiful waterway. For miles it skulks along through a modern industrial landscape: large featureless buildings with names that give away nothing of whatever's happening within, flanked by car parks. One of the few idiosyncratic – that is to say, human – features of this long industrial corridor is a tiny workmen's café, cheerfully offering breakfast, lunch and dinner, squeezed in between enormous factories.

But I digress...

Repetition with variation... The same old same old... dressed up in new clothes, given a fresh coat of paint, or make-up, taught the steps to a new dance...

We cruised out of Limehouse on a Monday morning. Our mooring was just a short walk, by the way, from The Grapes, which featured most memorably in Dickens's *Our Mutual* Friend: It was, he wrote,

> A tavern of dropsical appearance... long settled down into a state of hale infirmity. It had outlasted many a sprucer public house, indeed the whole house impended over the water but seemed to have got into the condition of a faint-hearted diver, who has paused so long on the brink that he will never go in at all.

Another digression. Mmm. It's going to be difficult writing this in less than a few thousand words.

Back to the Lee:

First we cruised up the navigation. We made heavy weather of the way up. The locks were formidable. The wind was cold.

Clouds glowered overhead. I huddled in a winter coat (in August!) at the tiller.

We passed through a gauntlet of narrowboats, home to hundreds of Londoners who daily make the trek from their homes on the water to dismal office blocks scattered across the city. I was screamed at by one woman who believed my bow-wave was larger than regulations dictated.

I nearly lost my Kindle when a gust of wind hurtling round the corner of a factory blasted across the stern, sending our guide to the waterways spinning into the canal where it promptly sank and smashing my entire library of ebooks to the stern deck.

Quarrels beset us. Should we have given ourselves more time to cruise to Bishop Stortford? Shouldn't we have lingered in London?

We moored at last in Broxbourne, a town whose ancient meaning is Badger's Stream, beneath towering horse chestnuts. We agreed that for now Bishop's Stortford was out of reach. We would turn around and go back. It seemed in some respects like a defeat.

And here beginneth the lesson, dear readers. For the journey back, although identical in every respect to the journey there, was at once different in every respect.

The sun shone with more enthusiasm than it has yet managed on our voyage. No one shouted at me. Gentle zephyrs caressed us. The canal at times seemed lined with elderflower in full and fragrant bloom. We met fellow narrowboaters whose natural friendliness charmed us. We struck up a conversation with a walker on the towpath who turned out to be... George R.R. Martin, author of *Songs of Ice and Fire* (aka *Game of Thrones*). I was about to tax him with his failure to deliver volume six of the saga, when he revealed that he'd been resident in England for the past fifty years... Not George at all, although he was the spitting image.

But that was the only disappointment of the return journey.

You might traverse the same territory, but everything is different: you look at the world through new eyes. It's the same story, but it's entirely novel. So take a bleak and desiccated idea, turn it on its head, or run it past you in reverse, and, lo, something entirely new can emerge.

Bilbo might have taken the same route home after his adventures with the dwarves, but since he was a very different hobbit on that return journey (travel-weary, stained by the malign influence of the ring, experienced in the bloody reality of battle) it was an entirely different experience.

And so it's possible to argue that all simple journeys – there and back again – are, in fact, epic.

3

THIRD VOYAGE

BRAUNSTON TO BEDFORD

THE MAGICAL POWER OF MOMENTUM

Some years have gone by and, after a number of other momentous journeys, we are about to set off on a voyage that will take us to our new mooring in Bedford.

Braunston is a charming village. It is the home of the so-called "cathedral of the canals", All Saints Church where boatmen in days of yore conducted their weddings, their baptisms and their funerals; as well as four pubs, to one or more of which celebrants presumably repaired after church for a pint or two.

But it's small and there are no coffee shops. It's also difficult to get to London. You have to catch a bus to Rugby, some miles to the north, before boarding a train for the capital. But then, thanks to the economic flavour of the day, austerity, the bus service was terminated.

So, we scoured the country for a marina within striking distance of London, that boasted at least two good coffee shops plus, if at all possible, a good bookstore, and a handful of halfway decent restaurants.

And, hey bingo, up popped Bedford. First, we explored it by water, and found that it appeared to possess all the features on our wish-list; then we confirmed our first impressions with a visit by car.

So now we were off.

By car, the journey from Braunston to Bedford takes something less than a hour. By canal and river... Well, that's an entire story in itself.

First you cruise south along the Grand Union Canal to the branch that leads down through seventeen locks to Northampton, where the canal ends and the navigable River Nene begins.

Sixty five miles to Peterborough.

The challenge now is to cross Cambridgeshire to pick up the River Great Ouse. This crossing is via what are called the Middle Levels – more or less a ditch not much wider than a couple of narrowboats. The Middle Levels drop below sea level, reminding you that this part of the country was developed originally by Dutch engineers imported in the seventeenth century to drain the Fens.

The Middle Levels intersect with the River Great Ouse at Denver, a giant sluice that dams the river. You motor up the river, passing Ely, St Ives, Huntingdon and St Neots before finally encountering the footbridge that crosses the entrance to Priory Marina.

By road, 44 miles. By canal and river, 180 miles. Travelling for a steady four hours a day, it'll take us 18 days, but since we often pause to explore the towns and villages – and what remains of the castle in which Mary Queen of Scots was beheaded on the orders of her wrathful cousin, Queen Elizabeth I – it'll take us all of a month to make the journey.

Most narrowboats on the United Kingdom's three thousand miles of waterways are powered by diesel engines, great hulking beasts that lurk under the rear decks of our vessels beating with muted ferocity.

But 'twas not always so. When the system of canals was first begun in the eighteenth century, all waterborne transport was drawn by horses. Which explains why, along every canal there runs a parallel towpath.

The narrowboats that carried the cargoes – coal, pottery, limestone, gravel – of the industrial revolution, weighed up to 50 tons. The question arises: how could a single horse tow a load of fifty tons? And the answer is, of course, that once a load of that size is moving through the water, it tends to keep moving. (I think Newton had something to do with this.) Its momentum is quite easily maintained.

Or take my own recent experience. I decided, just over a year ago, that a little weight lost would do me good, both in terms of my mobility – and my longevity. So naturally I did what all monomaniacs do, I established a spreadsheet. In one column, I noted the date. In the next, my weight, in the third, what I ate for breakfast, lunch and supper. I decided that on Tuesdays I would fast. I established goals. By the end of November, I wanted to have shed X kgs, by the end of December X+Y kgs, and so on.

After a couple of months I realised that I'd managed to do what the horses from the golden age of the English canals did routinely: I'd established a little momentum.

And the weight dropped off me. Now, fourteen months after the start of that particular voyage, I've lost 23 kgs. Depending on the size of the bag, that's somewhere between three and four bags of potatoes.

I'm astonished.

But I shouldn't be. Because the secret lies in momentum.

I was pondering these not-very profound verities when I came across something that Stephen King has written on this very same subject. Here's what he said:

> Once I start work on a project, I don't stop and I don't slow down unless I absolutely have to. If I don't write every day, the characters begin to stale off in my mind — they begin to seem like characters instead of real people. The tale's narrative

cutting edge starts to rust and I begin to lose my hold on the story's plot and pace.

Precisely. Let's go back to that lumbering cart horse. It's early morning. Mist covers the water. The ghost trees of winter loom across the waterway as the horse plods slowly along the canal path. At his tiller, the tillerman's attention drifts and he dozes. The horse takes note and slows, then pauses to snatch at some blades of winter wheat trespassing on the towpath. The narrowboat loses way.

The tillerman's father, brewing a pot of tea in the cabin, feels that loss of momentum. He throws open the hatch onto the stern deck.

"What the devil's going on?" he growls.

It takes the startled tillerman an age to coax the horse into motion once more, for the canal boat to gather momentum, and for order to be restored.

Write every day if you can manage it. Keep a record of your progress, however slow. Maintain your momentum for as long as possible, remembering how difficult it is to get going again when you falter.

ELENA FERRANTE'S SENSORIUM

This is a drum I have beaten before – and without doubt it is one I shall beat again, so if you object to percussion, put your hands over your ears and stop reading now.

The drum concerns detail – sensory detail – in one's writing. The world as we know it is a seamless blend of sight, sound, smell, taste and touch. It's impossible, in the real world, to imagine what it's like without this constant inpouring of sensory impressions.

We're three days down the Nene, having debouched from the Grand Union spur into the river at Northampton. The river is much narrower than the Thames, but possibly even more charming, with unexpected twists and turns that afford the alert tillerman to a constantly changing series of views and vistas.

There are not that many mooring spots. Last night, failing to find a suitable bank, we lashed ourselves to a couple of oaks and hoped that a river warden wouldn't demand we "move on".

I'm composing these thoughts in Patience which is moored to a landing stage at the foot of the garden of The King's Head public house in the village of Wadenhoe. We're tethered to the grassy bank in a tiny spur of the river developed specifically, we imagine, for just this purpose.

Behind us – or should I say, astern of us – runs the river,

dappled and dimpled by the wind. On my left, children are at play in the grounds of the pub, and their treble voices drift across to us.

The overwhelming sound, though, is of the soughing of the wind through the leaves of the tall trees about us: willow and poplar, beech and pine. The smells of the river, subtle and difficult to tease out – surround and infuse us. More intimately, I have a twinge in my back from a muscle I somehow pulled yesterday.

And that's just the beginning of it. If I dwelt on this, I could elaborate almost endlessly on the sights and sounds that envelop and inhabit me. All of these details would be significant to me. I recognise that that wouldn't be the case for anyone else. In fact, not one of these details would be of much interest to anyone else – unless they played an active role in a story.

Right. Now let's look at a barrelful of sensory detail deployed in what is without doubt a highly suspenseful story.

This is a passage drawn from Elena Ferrante's *My Brilliant Friend*, the first of her Neapolitan cycle.

She's describing her character, as a child, following her more courageous friend, as they climb the steps leading to the front door of the neighbourhood ogre, Don Achille:

> We kept to the side where the wall was, she two steps ahead, I two steps behind, torn between shortening the distance or letting it increase. I can still feel my shoulder inching along the flaking wall and the idea that the steps were very high, higher than those in the building where I lived. I was trembling, every voice was Don Achille creeping up behind us or coming down toward us with a long knife, the kind used for slicing open a chicken breast. There was an odour of sautéing garlic. Maria, Don Achille's wife, would put me in the pan of boiling oil, the children would eat me, he would suck my head the way my father did with mullets.

The senses of touch, sight, hearing, taste and smell are all invoked. And each of these details is vital in communicating the felt experience that the character's recalling. The details tell us a great deal about the fearful girl following in her friend's footsteps. And on top of that, they generate real tension.

Ferrante, in short, is inviting us into her sensorium so that we're able to share her fears and face with her the dangers the child her character once was, imagines.

There. I've beaten my drum, and now I'm done.

THE WRITER AS COLLECTOR

We met in a lock on the River Nene. He was a man in his sixties, with closely shorn white hair, beetling eyebrows over sharp eyes, and a firm hand on the tiller. His wife busied herself with mine, managing the slow process of closing the lock, filling it with water, opening the gates at the other end, then closing them behind us. The locks on the Nene are slow and cumbersome. We had twenty minutes. It was enough for a conversation.

He'd been a country policeman for thirty years. "Loved the life," he said, "from the days of my walking the beat in a little village near Ely, to being in charge of my own patch.

"What were the rules? Simple. I was a member of the community – important, that – given the authority of the Queen to protect the innocent and prosecute the guilty, without fear or favour.

"Nowadays, of course, things are different. There are more guidelines. There are more rules. There are specific goals, boxes to tick. Very different from when I was a constable on the beat."

Had he ever served in Soham, I asked him, the Cambridgeshire town that had been the site of the terrible murders of two young girls, Holly Wells and Jessica Chapman, in 2002, by the caretaker of the local school, Ian Huntley.

He'd served in Soham, but well before the murders. A friend had been in charge of the investigation. He paused a moment reflectively. "After they nailed Huntley," he said, "my friend retired. The investigation had shattered him."

Ahead of us the giant guillotine gates of the lock – on the Nene most of these are electrified – rose ponderously from the water.

"You go first," I said.

"Nice talking," he said, with a casual salute.

He gunned his diesel and pulled slowly out of the lock.

A day later, at another lock on the river, I found myself in an identical situation with a very similar looking man: sixties, grey haired, sharp-eyed. His immaculate diesel engine, visible through an open hatchway, gleamed.

I plied him with questions.

He'd been a uniformed customs official, he told me, for thirty years – just like my country policeman – investigating customs fraud and corruption. He'd taken a package when his section had been privatised. A few years later, in 2004, an old friend had invited him to South Africa to help him investigate customs fraud at Johannesburg's international airport. The job, he was told, would take no more than six weeks.

In fact, he stayed for a year.

"I worked in Pretoria," he said. "Wonderful experience. Except we made absolutely no progress with our investigation. The revenue service told us they didn't approve of the methods we used, and so weren't very co-operative. I didn't particularly mind. I was having a ball."

After a year, he returned to the UK, bought his narrowboat, and joined the ranks of a fleet of narrowboats known as continuous cruisers. They have no home base – although sometimes they'll take refuge in a marina for winter – but, as the name bestowed on them suggests, cruise the canal and river system continuously, stopping for no more than fourteen days at a stretch in any given mooring.

~

On our fifth or sixth day on the river, we moored against a meadow in Oundle, and tramped up to the Tap and Kitchen for a meal.

At the next table from us sat two old biddies, chatting about this and that. "Did you see, Mavis wasn't in church today," said one. "I knew, because I couldn't hear her coughing."

~

These are odd lots in the ongoing auction of a writer's life. Each contains a seed not simply of an idea for a possible story, but of a bit of texture to be added to any story...

The police detective shattered by his unsuccessful investigation into a gruesome murder, retires. Later he realises what he'd failed to investigate... or has an insight that provides a fresh lead... or stumbles across a clue. He returns to his old HQ and talks to his successor, who brushes him aside. He's old news, his insights lack any value, and in any event, the case has been shelved. So he goes home, defeated... before deciding to take up the investigation on his own...

The former customs investigator takes advantage of an invitation from an old buddy to help him root out corruption in a foreign land. He's a fish out of water. The politics are weird, the power relations incomprehensible. It's soon obvious who the fraudsters are. What's less obvious is why the institution he's supposed to be assisting is protecting the looters. Before he knows it, he's in over his head...

The old biddy is a bit like Sherlock Holmes, who noticed the fact that the dog *didn't* bark. She noticed that there *wasn't* that familiar rasping cough in the church. And this leads her into her own, cosy investigation into the disappearance of a friend she's known for over seventy years...

Writers are collectors. We interrogate people we encounter. We collect their stories. We squirrel them away. We like odd facts, we treasure bizarre anecdotes. We think: what if *this*, and what if *that*...?

And none of this is a chore. On the contrary, it's all gloriously entertaining.

Trish and I finished our meal with a couple of amarettos, before meandering back to Patience through the gathering twilight.

It had been another deeply satisfying day on the water. Next stop: Peterborough.

WILLOW HERB AND HOARY MULLEIN

I'm going to hark back now to our descent through the seventeen locks of the Rothersthorpe Flight on the Northampton Arm of the Grand Union Canal – the spur that connects the highway of the Grand Union that runs from London to Birmingham, with the River Nene and the lowlands of Cambridgeshire.

After the heavy double locks of the Grand Union, the Arm comes as a welcome relief. These locks are all single ones – just wide enough for a narrowboat to slip into. They fill quickly and empty quickly, and Trish has become adroit at leaping from one side of the lock to the other, saving herself the trouble of walking seventy feet down one side of the lock, and seventy feet up the other to open or close the lower gates.

The canal is not especially pretty – although, as always on the English canals, there is plenty to interest an enthusiast. We learned, for instance, that the Arm was built in 1815 – and saved from demolition by an enthusiastic company of amateurs in the 1960s and '70s.

And, of course, the banks of the canal are lined here, as almost always, with a great variety of trees, reeds and wildflowers.

By the time we were making this trip to Bedford, we'd been coming to Britain pretty well every summer for well over a decade, and over the period, sitting on the stern of Patience, my interest in the natural world has gradually evolved. At first, I simply absorbed all the greenery... The herons at every bend in the canal... The cathedral-like copses of sycamore and ash... The sublime views across the Yorkshire moors...

Those endless wildflowers...

I realised at some point that we had a book on British wildflowers on-board. From my perch, with the book in one hand, the tiller in the other, I started trying to identify some of them.

There was time, sitting in locks waiting for the water to gush out and lower us to the next level, to examine whatever blooms grew on the banks immediately alongside.

To be honest, though, I struggled to identify *any* of them. The drawings in the book, beautiful as they were, didn't seem to bear much resemblance to the flowers on the bank. We identified one species with certainty: the beautiful purple loosestrife.

And on our way down the canal to Northampton, sure enough, I spotted endless examples of purple loosestrife.

But I was strangely dissatisfied. Here we were, surrounded by endless examples of wildflowers, and I was able to name just one of them.

Pathetic.

So we kept a weather-eye open for a better book – and found one in Peterborough: *Harrap's Wild Flowers* which covers 934 species of wild flowers, shrubs and trees in Britain and Ireland, the blurb tells us. Multiple photographs are devoted to each species.

After a day or two spent admiring the great flotillas of swans that cruise endlessly up and down the river in Peterborough, we motored down river a mile or so, then turned onto what are called the Middle Levels.

This is an exceedingly modest waterway. It hardly qualifies as a canal. It's narrow and shallow. In places you can feel the flat bottom of your boat – narrowboats don't have keels – brush against underwater vegetation.

You're cruising in pretty close proximity to the plant life on both sides of you, and it was at last possible for me to match pictures in my glossy new book with the flowers on the banks.

Willowherb. In such pink profusion that it was an embarrassment *not* knowing what it was. In Whittlesey I snatched a flower growing out of a wall alongside the river. Red valerian.

White and yellow waterlilies lined the margins of long stretches of the canal. Arrowhead dotted the water's surface, with their distinctive but less flashy pink and purple flowerets.Wild teasels populated some sections of the bank in dense clusters.

And then suddenly, the willowherb was supplanted by endless stands of Indian or Himalayan balsam, great bushes of pink and white and purple blossom.

It's the custom – now not universally observed – to tip the lock-keepers who preside over two of the three locks on the Middle Levels. The last lock, before we reached the intersection with the River Great Ouse, is called Marmont Priory Lock. On the day we passed through it, there was no sign of the lock-keeper. Our route maps warned us, however, that she is something of a legend, and is not to be crossed.

So although she was not there to ease our passage, we dutifully left three pounds on the side of the lock to acknowledge our fealty.

At the point at which we entered the Ouse from the Middle Levels, at Salter's Lode, the river is tidal. The little fleet of boats – both narrowboats and cruisers – that had gathered there waiting for high tide, took instruction from the lock-keeper, who urged caution on the two hundred metre stretch from his lock to the Denver Sluice, which tames the River Great Ouse.

"There are shallow sandbanks," he warned us. "So follow the boat ahead of you, go to neither port not starboard, keep to the channel."

We kept to the channel, gunning our motor to overcome the effects of the tidal currents already opposing us. The boat ahead of us veered off to one side, briefly going aground on the dreaded sandbank but then, thanks to the surging current, shook itself free, and continued on to the huge sluice gates and lock at Denver.

We continued our journey on the calm waters of the Ouse above Denver Sluice, until Ely Cathedral, as impressive as any we've seen anywhere, appeared to starboard. Ely was once an island – the island of eels – and the cathedral was built almost a thousand years ago on a hill that dominated the Fens.

We paused briefly, but then pressed on to St Ives, my search to identify wildflowers continuing. By the time we got there, we'd seen hoary mullein, creeping cinquefoil, silverweed, marsh woundwort, orange balsam, branched bur-reed, flowering rush, cotton thistle, common mallow and endless stretches of a variety of that most humble of all water plants, duckweed: greater duckweed, fat duckweed, ivy-leaved duckweed...

And as we worked our way further up the river past Hemingford Grey and Huntingdon I spotted all the flowers we'd so far identified, and named them to myself, endlessly, as a way of committing them all firmly to memory. And as I did so, I realised that I was seeing flowers that had been invisible to me on our journey down the Nene. The words I was now able to command isolated and identified specific flowers that had previously passed in a blur.

And so I stumbled on another example of the power of specificity.

Write: "He walked through a meadow, conscious of the flowers spread in sweet profusion around him" and we might shrug. But if we'd written: "He walked through a meadow filled with wild teasels and great banks of willowherb," we'll sense that this is a realer, more authentic world, full, not of generics – but sewn from the cloth of a more closely observed reality.

Name things and we bring them forth into the world of our

fiction (or fact). The more specific we can be, the more convincing that world will be.

Take it from me, as I open my Harraps in search of the name of a little yellow flower that I plucked from between two thistles at our mooring at St Neots, just one day's cruising from our destination.

ON THE MARGINS OF THE RIVER, A LESSON FOR US ALL

Herons are long-legged fresh-water and coastal birds which live on a varied diet of small fish, crustacea, frogs and aquatic insects. On both rivers and canals, we pass herons regularly as we slowly putter by in Patience.

Our cruise, now in its fourth week, to Bedford, at the extreme end of navigation on the River Great Ouse, has been trouble-free – although en route we had to make panicked trips to London to acquire Italian visas for our Venetian writing retreat.

But the days spent in London queueing for Schengen visas, stressful as they were, were soon mended by our time on the river.

Over the convoluted 180-mile, 87-lock journey, we've spotted upwards of a hundred herons quietly fishing at the riverside.

They're so skinny that they seem two-dimensional, grey and blue shadows without substance, perched sometimes in trees above the water, more often in the shallows along the margins of the watercourse. They stand with their heads hunched deep between their shoulders. They appear to take no notice of the slowly approaching narrowboat, but then, most often, launch themselves into the air, dip down for a moment, before their wings power them aloft in a great sweep over the meadow behind them.

But sometimes a heron will ignore the boat and continue to scrutinise the water with fixed concentration. Then it lunges at something in the water and a split second later raises its head with a minnow wriggling in its beak. The bird tosses its head back, swallows its snack, and resumes its solitary vigil, eyes fixed once more on the water.

On the upper reaches of the River Great Ouse on a tidal section just up-river from Earith, we passed a bird that looked like a miniature version of the standard heron. Standing, its head sinks, like the heron's, between its shoulders. In flight, its silhouette is identical to the heron's. But it is, as I say, much smaller than its larger relative – and a pure and absolute white. It is, not surprisingly, a member of the heron family, but is in fact called a little egret.

The greatest point of difference between the two birds, though, lies not in their size and colour, but in their feeding habits. The heron stands still as a statue and waits for its prey to swim by. The little egret, by contrast, actively pursues its lunch, dancing with raised wings through the shallows, stabbing its long harpoon-like beak at fish that its feet have disturbed, leaping into the air and splashing down, that beak darting down with startling speed...

Both varieties of heron earn a substantial living. I watched a little egret splash through the shallows for fifty or sixty metres as it kept pace with Patience, and in that time it caught and swallowed half a dozen titbits, the largest of which was a tiddler two inches in length.

I've watched dozens of herons spear fish of various sizes, sometimes in quick succession, and gobble them down.

My point?

Well, it's a small one, but it's intended to reassure. Having spent my apprentice years in the television industry, I write very fast. I'm happy to give myself a target of two thousand words a day – and when I'm really flying (skipping along the margins of my literary river) I can write four or five thousand words a day.

There are many writers who work in this way. Joyce Carol Oates in her heyday wrote forty or fifty *pages* a day. Karl Ove Knausgaard, whose autobiographical magnum opus, *My Struggle*, took Scandinavia (and the world) by storm some years ago, wrote thirty or forty pages a day.

But at the other end of the spectrum, there are writers who consider two or three hundred words a day a satisfying output. They stand patiently waiting for the right word to swim by, and spear it with an authoritative flourish.

So whatever you are – slow and steady, fast and impulsive – know that all that matters is the succulence of the fish you catch.

Happy fishing.

THE SURPRISING, THE ACCURATE, THE PERFECT PHRASE

It's just a five- or six-hour cruise from St Neots to Priory Marina in Bedford, a very pleasant journey between trees and fields. Occasionally the river widens a little, but for the most part it traces a narrow, winding path through the undulating landscape of central Bedfordshire.

Changing your permanent moorings is always a little nerve-wracking, we've found. We'd inspected Priory Marina, as I've said, but we had no idea, as we chugged these last few miles towards our new home, whether we'd find either the marina or the town congenial.

I sat at the tiller weighing these imponderables. Puttering along at three or at most four miles an hour encourages you to cultivate a certain philosophical outlook on the world. You consider, so to speak, the lilies of the field, and what effect observing them as you slowly pass by has on what has become known these days as your mental health.

But occasionally, philosophical reflection palls, and you turn to other means of entertainment – chief of which is the radio.

So, on the final stretch of our long journey to Bedford, I tuned in to the Book of the Week on Radio Four.

The book, it turned out, was called *Spirals in Time: The Secret Life and Curious Afterlife of Seashells* by Dr Helen Scales.

It was an odd sort of book, I thought, to be serialising. But then my attention was caught by a single phrase that was so surprising, so accurate, so perfect, that I thought I'd make it the subject of today's meditation.

The subject was the symbolism of shells. Scales was describing the extraordinary power of the cowrie, as currency and as sexual symbol. I learned that the classical Chinese character for money originated as a stylised drawing of a Maldivian cowrie shell.

And then she dropped her perfect bombshell. "So many people," she wrote, "have picked up a cowrie shell, turned it over and seen a lengthwise dark opening like a corrugated smile that reminded them of female genitalia."

"... A corrugated smile." Think about it for a moment. Remember the last time you held the smooth weight of a cowrie shell in your hand. Remember running your finger across that series of bumps at the entrance to the shell's mysterious chamber.

A corrugated smile. Original. Accurate. Perfect. Like Oscar Wilde, I can hear myself saying, I wish I'd said that. (And I can just about hear the echo of the man who said, sotto voce, "You will, Oscar, you will.")

In our writing, we strive to think of phrases that are as apt as this one. And when we do, we have every right to feel a sense of deep satisfaction.

"Trish," I called out, not to draw her attention to the final moments of the Book of the Week, but to the lock that lay ahead. Cardington Lock is just a mile from our destination. She popped out onto the bow, leapt onto the landing stage below the lock, and set about emptying the lock.

After we'd threaded our way beneath the ominous guillotine at the head of the lock, I picked Trish up, and we began the last lap of our journey, one that had taken us just short of four weeks. She joined me for the final stretch on the deck.

"There it is. The finishing line." I pointed ahead to a barely discernible break in the treeline on our right. Approaching the turn into the marina, I gave a definitive toot on our horn to warn a boat that might have been preparing to shoot out onto the river, and pushed the tiller hard left.

We had arrived.

4

THE RIVER GREAT OUSE

BEDFORD

THE SECRET IN THE IRON-BOUND CHEST

Bedford, our new home, possesses, as I've said before, many charms and advantages. What I hadn't anticipated was discovering that among its attractions was the curious history of an institution called the Panacea Society. It was a millenarian religious group, founded in 1919 which followed the teachings of a nineteenth century seer or prophetess whose singular legacy was an iron-bound chest stuffed full, she said, of prophecies.

The founder of the society, Mabel Barltrop, was the widow of an Anglican clergyman. The Panacea Society didn't attract thousands of adherents, but it did sign up enough wealthy members for it to establish itself in the town in a substantial way. By the 1930s, seventy members of the society had clustered together in community in Bedford, buying properties and funding the construction of a society HQ.

What has any of this to do with writing, you may well ask? Well, naturally, curiosities of all kinds should be of interest to any writer. We're all curious creatures, no? And the thought of a sealed, iron-bound box, a number of prophecies, a secretive, committed group of believers – well, it all sounds rather Indiana Jones-ish, or even Dan Brown-ish, doesn't it?

But there's more, people... Let's first take a step or two back, and examine, not just the curious features of the Panacea Society, but the reasons for its success – and its ultimate demise – and how these teach lessons instructive to writers.

Let's begin with that sealed casket. The original prophetess, Joanna Southcott, was a prolific predictor of the future. There's no record of what those predictions were, but presumably her reputation was built on at least some success. But her juiciest prophecies were, it was believed, consigned to the box, and sealed.

That box, and the tantalising promise of its contents, were used strategically by Mrs Barltrop to attract adherents. Because the burning question was, what had the legendary Joanna Southcott prophesied?

The sealed box is familiar to every screenwriter. It is, in the lingo of film theory, a MacGuffin* – a mystery which all who heard about wanted solved.

Mrs Barltrop's iron-bound chest and its mysterious contents created instant intrigue. It generated suspense. A petition was circulated in the early 1930s that was signed by 100 000 people: open the box, it cried. Everyone wanted to know what was in the box!

So, the question is, why didn't they simply open the damn thing?

Because Mrs Barltrop was a clever woman. She knew that if they opened the box, the mysteries would be solved, the questions would be answered, the suspense would be relieved.

What she did was stipulate under what conditions the box could be opened and she built them into the founding rules of her order. Only if twenty four bishops of the Church of England gathered together in Bedford could the box be legitimately opened. Some of the funds contributed by believers was used to construct a building designed specifically to house the conclave of the bishops. It was named, appropriately, the Bishops' House. One of the chief objectives of the society was to persuade those bishops to agree to meet in the Bishops' House for that purpose.

Advertisements were placed in the local and national press, imploring the Church to heed the society's call. Personal appeals to the then Archbishop of Canterbury followed.

Naturally, the Church of England gave the society a very polite middle finger.

And then, rumours circulated that the box had, in fact been opened – and inside all that had been found was "a broken horse pistol and a lottery ticket".

Without any prospect of the box's being opened (if, indeed, it hadn't already been opened) the Panacea Society's bright star waned and its membership dwindled – although its heart continued to beat, albeit falteringly, for a surprisingly long time. Its last member died in 2012 whereupon its assets – some millions of pounds – were converted into a charitable trust, a museum was opened, (you'll find it in Newnham Road, close to the town centre) and the once fervent cult, became an historical curiosity.

If you have a big secret at the heart of your narrative, you have to make sure of at least three things: one, that you don't let the cat out of the bag prematurely; two, that you persuade your readers that at some stage before the end of your story the secret *will* be revealed; and, three, that the secret will have been worth waiting for.

You could bear these lessons in mind when devising your next nail-biting thriller – or, if you're truly ambitious with megalomaniac tendencies, you could use them in constructing your very own cult.

So, after all, the Panacea Society (which, by the by, believed that Bedford was the original site of the Garden of Eden) did leave a legacy worth recounting.

* Here, from Mr W, a pithy definition: In fiction, a MacGuffin, (sometimes McGuffin or maguffin) is a plot device in the form of some goal, desired object, or another motivator that the protagonist pursues, often with little or no narrative explanation.

EVERY GENIUS BEGINS AS AN APPRENTICE

Some people have a kind of preternatural understanding of story structure, an inborn ability to create memorable characters and a clear appreciation of the need for detail, tension and conflict in their narrative.

Lucky them.

Most of us are less gifted. Between us and anything half-way decent lie years of trial and error (mostly error); scenes that have to be written and rewritten so often that we come to hate the blasted things; deliberation so self-conscious that, to begin with, everything feels stilted and false.

The greats, in whatever field, stride effortlessly through narratives that appear flawless, paintings in which every brushstroke is perfectly placed and perfectly executed; concerti of astonishing balance and beauty.

Cast your mind over all the masters, in whatever field: Beethoven, Leonardo, Shakespeare – and Turner.

The Higgins Art Gallery in Bedford, just a hop and a skip from our marina and round the corner from both the castle mound and the Panacea Society Museum, advertised with some excitement the fact that they were hosting an exhibition of drawings and paintings of the young J.M.W. Turner.

The exhibition is on a tour of Britain to celebrate the acquisition by Oxford's Ashmolean Museum of Turner's celebrated painting of the city's High Street.

It is a masterly work of art. It seems to confirm everything we know of artistic genius. The lines are true and clear. The perspective is masterful. The composition is pleasing. The city's air of light and learning is apparent in, yes, every brushstroke.

So, our case rests. The greats just have it. The rest of us have to learn it.

But hang on a mo. Our guide at the Higgins pointed to the prodigious effort that Turner had made in order to master perspective in the first place. He informed us that Turner spent four years preparing for his inaugural lecture as professor of perspective at the Royal Academy – but that he then managed, quite royally, to screw it up. His subject was, naturally: how to master perspective. At least one member of the hundreds that crowded in to hear the great man expatiate on his theme said he came away utterly confused.

Well, I suppose all that proves is that he was a terrible communicator. But look at those lines in the Oxford High Street painting! Doesn't that establish beyond doubt that he had an instinctive understanding of the subject, whatever his shortcomings in the lecture hall?

Before we start celebrating Turner's emergence as a prodigy consider the 30 000 preparatory sketches that he made before he committed himself to his early architectural studies. That gave him ample opportunity to err – and revise. To rinse, and repeat. To fail, and fail again.

Or remind yourself of the fact that, at the age of thirteen and fourteen he was learning the skills of an architectural draughtsman, and later studied under another renowned master of perspective, Thomas Malton.

We can conclude that, Turner, although unquestionably a creative genius, had to apply himself to the underlying skills and techniques of his craft before he could bring off his signature paintings.

So when next you look at some of those astonishing paintings of his later life – *Rain, Steam and Speed*, *The Fighting Temeraire* and dozens of others – remember that he began where we all begin – as an apprentice.

SATURDAY MORNING IN THE SUN

We met at La Piazza in St Paul's Square, just a stone's throw from the river, for coffee. The sun was shining. The crowds of people browsing for vegetables at the Saturday market were dressed for summer. Every table at the little open-air Italian coffee shop was occupied.

In short, it was a lovely late spring day in Bedford.

Over coffee, Trish and I decided on what we'd do at our allotment this afternoon.

I showed her the sketch I'd made of the growing frames I intended to build.

"They're for the pumpkins, right?" she said.

"One for pumpkins, one for the gems." Gem squashes are an exotic South African import whose seeds we'd smuggled into the country last year. We've got half a deckful back at the houseboat* of vigorous seedlings of both the gems and two varieties of pumpkin waiting to be planted out.

"What have you got planned?" I asked.

"Strim the pathways, weed the brassica cage – and I've had an idea for the bed between the brassica cage and the road. I think we should turn it into a mini-meadow."

It's a great idea. We've got the seeds for a medley of wildflowers that should flourish over the summer months.

Trish went off then to collect our car which was in for a service, and I briefly considered which route home I'd take on my mobility scooter. You can choose the road along the Embankment, which is pleasant enough. The Embankment is the jewel in the crown of the town, established by Victorian town planners, and featuring impressive avenues of willow and plane.

Or you can take the less travelled path on the far side of the river.

No contest.

This route runs along the river – that's the River Great Ouse, as you should know by now – before joining the old railway track, now converted into a cycle and pedestrian path that leads all the way to Sandy, a nearby town.

At the end of spring, it is flanked on either side by huge stands of cow parsley, known also, more grandly, as Queen Anne's lace, which waves in the breeze, parting occasionally to reveal glimpses of the river beyond and, at one point, of a swan indolently drifting across its surface, one foot tucked comfortably on his back; and beyond it, his mate, sitting on her clutch of eggs.

I paused frequently to take photographs of wildflowers along the margins of the path. In the old days, I'd consult *Harrap's Wild Flowers* to identify them. Today, my phone does it for me. I'm not sure that this is a good thing. It's as though I'm outsourcing my research...

Cow parsley I knew, of course, but I took several pictures of it anyway because it is, in its lush profusion, quite beautiful. And it releases a subtle but distinctive scent of honey.

I snapped a very common wildflower, one of the first I'd ever identified on an early voyage on Patience: red campion it's called, a small but vibrant pink bloom with five bifurcated petals. I learned from my phone that it's also called red catchfly. Then I spotted an even more modest flower, almost concealed among the leaves of its parent. It's ground ivy.

And a few metres on, a brilliant head of hogweed florets.

In quick succession I photographed three members of the geranium family the first of which was a French crane's-bill. The flower itself is a pale blue on which is scrawled in red a sketch of *another* flower. The second was its cousin, the pink hedgerow cranesbill; and the third, just a few metres on, was the humble small flowered cranesbill.

I hope I haven't stretched your patience. What I'm trying to convey to you is the almost sublime experience of working my slow way back to our lake, each stop along the way offering something new, something exquisite.

By the time I reached the graceful arched pedestrian bridge that leads onto the old railway track, I can say that I was about as happy as one can be. An intimate voyage of discovery through the natural world, we all acknowledge, can have that effect.

When I was halfway over the bridge, an old codger on a bicycle wobbled onto the other end. I came to a stop to reduce the chances of a collision. He had a great bush of a moustache and was neatly tucked into a tight jacket, which he kept buttoned.

As he passed, he said: "At least the sun is shining."

Well, if ever you needed a single line of dialogue to plunge you to the heart of a character, that was it. That's often *all* you need, in easing someone new into a story: a single significant detail to do with their appearance, or their attitude, or their mood. "At least the sun is shining," does it for me.

P.S. There's something else I want to point out. I don't think the old guy's remark would have had the dramatic effect I was seeking, without the set-up that preceded it.

* A year after we joined the live-aboard community in Priory Marina, we bought a houseboat (we call her Impatience). Patience remains moored at a nearby pontoon.

WHAT BEING A HERON CAN TEACH US

We're now living on that houseboat at the end of a pontoon in a lake fed by the River Great Ouse on the outskirts of Bedford. We are virtually surrounded by water. Birds of various species inhabit the lake. From the deck on which we take our morning coffee we can gaze deep into the clear water where thickets of water plants rise like phantoms from the floor – and a number of fish species dart and glide through the forest.

Why this extended introduction to our world? Well, because when three large carp startled me recently by ramming the wall just below our study window, I was, like a character from a Chinese fable, sucked into the contemplation of what life as a fish, or more specifically, as a carp, might be like.

Silly, I know, but suddenly I experienced the rush of water over my scales, felt thoughts and speculations drain from my consciousness, realised that my world consisted now of sensation only: the water, the presence at my side of a couple of my kind, murky reaches stretching out on all sides of me. I am a muscle and a mouth, and I'm hungry.

Life as a goose is a very different proposition. You'll need to choose your species, because different species have different outlooks on life. To inhabit the mind of a Canada goose requires a passionate response to your fellows. It's either love or loathing, I'm afraid, but as a Canada goose you'll fight or frolic with equal abandon.

There's a famous writing prompt that challenges writers to write from the perspective of a bat. You can see the difficulties involved. You live in a world of sound. You hunt relentlessly, eating on the move, zigzagging, plunging, reversing abruptly to intersect with your fluttering targets.

Why is this much more than a childish game? Well, it's because it pierces to the essence of the fiction-writing project. This is what you're required to do every time you sit down to write a scene.

You have to sink into the consciousness of your perspective character, feel with his nerves, observe his world, think in terms of his fears and trepidations, seek out the objects of desire that *he* favours. You have to draw on his vocabulary, his memories, even his perversities.

If you don't do this, then to some degree or other you're writing him from the outside. However good an observer you are, however fine a writer, there'll be a dimension missing. And we, your readers, will sense that deficit and the effect on us will be to introduce some distance between us and your character. We will, in short, become less engaged.

We live, as I say, at the end of a long pontoon, from which a number of jetties protrude, like branches from a stem. To each of these jetties a houseboat will, in due course, be tethered. We're alone for the moment because Covid-19 has put a halt to the marina's efforts to market these moorings. But in due course we expect to be just one of a community of twelve identical houseboats.

And so, instead of human neighbours, we have geese – not just Canada geese, but Egyptian geese and a solitary greylag.

The Canada geese are by far in the majority. In fact, their flock is the largest of all on our lake. I say "flock" but actually the Canada geese consist of a number of warring factions; small colloquies in search, apparently, of opportunities for disputation with other groups. When they meet, they engage in disorderly debate that frequently disintegrates into physical violence with one or more geese attacking another, both on the water and in the air.

I'd thought on the basis of my early encounters with the geese that that's all they were: fairly disreputable, ill-tempered creatures quite capable of murder in pursuit of their disagreeable agenda.

But prolonged observation has caused me to revise this opinion.

This is what I saw just a week or so ago: a goose was standing, as these water birds are wont to do, on one leg on one of the decks protruding from the pontoon. A half hour or so before, his companion had leapt into the water and paddled off in search, I imagined, of a brawl. But now there it was, returning along the broad avenue of water that runs down the middle of the lake between ranks of narrow and wide-beamed boats. My bird, the one left standing on one leg, gave a loud honk – had I mentioned that that's their characteristic call? – and leapt in his turn into the water.

He paddled energetically towards the other honking furiously and I thought, oh, oh – here's trouble. As he approached, his honking grew more and more intense, ranging in tone from deep, foghorn rumbles to contralto cries of what I realised was... delight.

These were mates. Canada geese I learned, are monogamous and mate for life, and here were greeting each other with unalloyed pleasure, what I was witnessing was a kind of renewal of vows. *He* honked, *she* murmured in basso profundo, and the two of them circled eyeing each other with undisguised joy.

But in addition to the geese, we have mallards aplenty, busy creatures who bustle about the lake, and pause to sun themselves on our walkways. We have the occasional coot migrant with his characteristic high whistle of a call.

And we have the most distinguished visitor of all, a haughty heron who stalks very deliberately along the pontoon with an air of slightly injured dignity. To be a heron for an afternoon is my next project. I anticipate that it'll require a degree of anxious caution, but above all I'll need to encourage within myself an immense reservoir of patience.

HOW I FELL OUT OF LOVE WITH SWANS

This is a story about how a gauzy attachment to a stereotype was shattered by the facts.

On our travels on the canals and rivers of England, we have encountered hundreds, perhaps thousands of swans. On the Thames we often found ourselves nosing our way through flotillas of the birds sailing regally on the dark waters, admiring their grace, their serenity and their parenting skills.

In Stoke-on-Trent, we watched a swan shepherd her newly hatched brood to the water for their first swim. On a flight of locks in Worcestershire in mid-winter, against the backdrop of a frozen dawn landscape, a swan beat its way heavily up the course of the locks with a whomp, whomp, whomp of its wings, leaving in our minds an unforgettable image. On the River Trent a swan passed by our narrowboat surrounded by a cluster of thirteen cygnets, apparently undaunted by the prospect of raising a brood the size, almost, of a team of rugby players.

Swans are in England nominally the property of the monarch and two of the ancient livery companies of the City of London. Every summer three skiffloads of "swan uppers" move in stately procession up the Thames counting the population of swans, ringing new additions to the flock and checking generally on their health. We've watched the swan uppers, dressed in traditional kit, at work.

On Priory Lake we've got to know the two resident swans. They make the rounds each day, visiting narrowboats and houseboats to politely request a handout. We oblige. Last year we bought a twenty-kilogram bag of swan food – pellets designed to meet the nutritional needs of the birds – and dispense handfuls of these whenever "our" swans appear at our door. If we don't immediately respond, they knock impatiently at the floor-to-ceiling window that overlooks the water.

In our first year on the lake, the pair failed to produce any progeny.

In the second, the female laid seven eggs. A couple were predated either by opportunistic crows or by an otter who scouts the area for eggs left unguarded by any one of the many water bird species. Several others proved unviable and didn't hatch. Eventually two eggs did hatch, but after just one maiden voyage, one of those chicks disappeared. We conjectured that one of the large pike that cruise the lake had snatched it from below.

But the survivor flourished, and by autumn had grown into a fine specimen, still in its pearly adolescent plumage, but independent and, of course, like all of its kind, quite, quite beautiful. He disappeared late in the year. We imagined that he'd struck out on his own as young adults do everywhere.

This year, our pair proudly produced nine chicks. The convoy cruises about the lake guarded jealously by both parents, one in the van, the other in the rear. The adults see off any other birds they judge threaten their offspring. When we're on our kayak, we take care never to paddle between the parents and their cygnets in case the former take umbrage.

All of this is demonstration of the fact that we have, in common with millions of others, enjoyed something of a love affair with swans, observing their behaviour, admiring their quirks, loving the sound as they whoosh past on whistling wings.

And then two weeks ago a neighbour on our lake confided

that he hated swans. He made this declaration with such venom that, shocked, we asked him why.

"They're greedy, cruel and vicious," he said. "The cob killed his son last year. Probably imagined that his mother had been having it off with some passing itinerant and that it wasn't his boy at all." Our neighbour had witnessed the fight that led to the death of the half-grown swan and described in graphic detail that fight to the death.

We hadn't realised that had been the fate of the single offspring we'd grown to love so much.

And it's true that swans attack without mercy any birds that irritate or annoy them. Our big cob has taken a particular dislike to one of the Canada geese on the lake, and hounds him continually, following him interminably and ultimately forcing him to fly to safety in the lake that adjoins ours.

I've started noticing that the adults snatch up the pellets we scatter on the water's surface before their cygnets have a chance to feed.

So now, when I watch the cob sailing down the central channel of our lake, serene as the rising sun, his wings curled in exquisite symmetry above his back, I can't help reflecting that not only is he beautiful – he is also greedy, cruel, vicious and guilty of filicide.

What am I to make of my exploded assumptions? Well, I suppose it's an old lesson that we have to learn repeatedly, and perhaps we never do entirely absorb: there's no such thing as a hero without feet of clay. The things, the people, the institutions we admire for their adherence to some shining ideal are, in the end, flawed.

We can love our swans and our role models, with the knowledge that inevitably they will disappoint us. But then, when the gloss has faded, we must find it possible, still, despite everything, to restore our belief in those aspects of our idols that have earned our respect and, yes, our love.

And this is also the challenge we face as writers. When we

create our protagonists, we can't simply portray them as paragons of virtue. They are, after all, human – and like swans, humans are complex and contradictory characters. It's not always possible – in fact, perhaps it's *never* possible – to square the circle of that complexity. Our guy is good – but he's also bad. At the same time.

So, while I might have fallen out of love with our swans, somehow, the love affair persists.

LEARN TO FLY WITH THE CYGNETS OF PRIORY MARINA

The cygnets of Priory Marina lake are learning to fly. Every day for the past week or two, seven of the offspring of our resident swans have taken to flapping their way up and down the central channel.

Sometimes the flying lessons are initiated by one of the parents. The adult stretches out its neck, its great wings beat the air, hitting the water with each downward thrust in a series of rapid explosions that send droplets of water scattering. Gathering speed, it rises from the water until its feet, awkward on land, run nimbly along the lake's surface.

Now, the adult swans of course use this form of locomotion – half running, half flying – to launch themselves into the air. But just as frequently, they use it simply to hurry from one end of the lake to the other. It's much faster than their usual stately glide.

By they also, quite deliberately, use it to teach their kids the rudiments of flying – and, presumably, to strengthen their flight muscles. So up and down the lake every day they go. Either the adults or the cygnets start the exercise, but then they're followed by the others who, one at a time, and sometimes two or even three of them together, race down the channel looking as if they're about to soar into the air. At the last moment, however, they abandon any pretensions they might have had to taking off, and slew to a stop, raising a mini-tsunami as they do so.

The day before I sat down to write this piece, one cygnet briefly rose out of the water altogether for a few seconds. Its feet broke contact with the silvery-green surface. It was a Kitty Hawk moment, true flight seemed imminent... But it was not to be, and the cygnet settled back into the water, waggled its tail, and serenely began plucking pondweed from the depths.

Within the next few days, I imagine, one of the cygnets will lift off and soar effortlessly above the willows, sycamores and alders that surround the lake. Once one has achieved this feat, the others will swiftly follow.

It's impossible, naturally, to plumb the consciousness of non-human animals.* We can have no idea what goes on in an avian brain. And yet I can't help imagining the sense of triumph – or perhaps surprise – that a swan feels on first breaking free from the surly bonds of earth.

As writers we can learn at least one lesson from these nursery flights of cygnets preparing for their aerial existence.

Persistence pays.

When our cygnets first began practising, I'm sure they had no idea at all that it was possible to fly. And yet, with utmost diligence, they set about doing the exercises that would enable them to ascend into the heavens. Again and again and again they charged down the lake, endlessly repeating the same moves, going a little faster, increasing in confidence, each time.

And then, at some point, they'll find themselves aloft. They'll tuck their feet in, stretch their necks out, rise above the trees and plunge into the sun-split clouds...**

Just as we might, when we've absorbed the craft, have paid our dues and are able, finally, to take our place as proud members of the writing fraternity.

. . .

* I'm not sure that this is true of all birds, but some species at least are able to send half their brains to sleep at a time, so that they're always at least partly alert to the dangers of the night (or the day, for nocturnal species). Now, try imagining that...

** You might have noticed that I've borrowed a couple of phrases from John Gillespie Magee's poem, *High Flight*.

IT'S WHAT OUR WORLD IS MADE OF

In a little more than a month, we will be hunting for truffles in Istria during the course of our Croatian writing retreat. It'll demand a keen sense of smell, I imagine – although I'm pretty sure the noses that sniff them out will be canine, or perhaps porcine, and not human.

Today, Trish and I walked our neighbour, Caroline's dog, Aggie, down the old railway track – now a bicycle path – that runs alongside our marina to the embankment in Bedford. It's a lovely walk that takes you under an overhang of sycamores and planes, ash and horse chestnut. On either side of the path lie banks of wildflowers and nettles. Of course, in late autumn the flowers have fled, although here and there you'll spot a desiccated blackberry.

But what assails you as you stroll down the green tunnel of vegetation are the smells: of earth, of decaying leaf mould, of autumnal dampness. It's easy to imagine networks of fungi underground transmitting their elemental messages from tree to tree, from copse to copse.

Aggie, a fine and silent hound (she only barks at swans) stops frequently, as dogs do, to savour the olfactory evidence of previous perambulating canines – although what excites her most are the traces of the squirrels and rabbits that she detects en route.

It's a pity that dogs can't write, because if they could they'd give us insight into a world in which the senses play a far greater role than they do in ours.

Imagine a consciousness in which words don't exist – but an infinite range of smells tells you all you need to know: a large, aggressive dog passed this way just minutes ago; a squirrel is perched somewhere in that tree; a rabbit nibbled beneath this patch of honesty several hours ago...

Our senses might not be as acute as our pets' – but we must do what we can with what we have, and report, in our writing, on all the sensations we experience: the heady perfume of wild jasmine, the plash of water at the weir, the gleam of sunlight that intermittently penetrates the canopy above us, the taste of rain-drops on our tongue, the rough contours of an old oak's trunk against a trailing hand.

It's what our world is made of. It's how we make the world of story come alive.

IN PRAISE OF LEAF MOULD

On Friday mornings, Trish, our friend and neighbour Caroline and I have taken to spending the morning in a bistro called Bridges in the centre of Bedford. There we have coffee, a breakfast (typically poached eggs, spinach, bacon, perhaps a sausage and a couple of slices of halloumi) and we work until perhaps noon.

Then we saunter home. By "saunter" I mean, Trish and Caroline are on foot, and I am on my mobility scooter. Our invariable companion on these adventures is Aggie, Caroline's extraordinarily well-behaved rescue dog I introduced you in the last piece.

The journey home takes us along the Victorian Embankment on the River Great Ouse – in flood at the moment thanks to the rain that has been lashing this country for what sometimes feels like the last decade or so. It is a charming walk. We're accompanied by flotillas of swans sailing up and down the swollen waters of the river, unperturbed by the speed of the stream.

Then we duck down along a trail that leads under Longholme Way and turn onto the arrow-straight pathway that follows the line of the railway between Oxford and Cambridge, ripped out by tweezer-lipped bureaucrats in the 1960s. There are now proposals to rebuild the connection between the two cities at vast expense.

These final few hundred metres are flanked by trees – on our right, a ditch beyond the treeline, and then the chain link fence surrounding the marina; on our left a bank, a band of trees, and one of the many arms of the Ouse.

We're walking along the tarred path. "Listen," I say. These are the elements of the soundscape:

The rattle and clatter of my scooter wheels on the tar. The hum of distant traffic. The swish-swish of Trish and Caroline's raincoats. The slight susurration of a breeze passing through the bare branches of the trees on either side of us. The repeated and piercing note of a great tit. The raucous kraak of a heron winging its way high above us. The croo-croo of doves. The sluice of water hurrying down the river on our left. The faint pad of Aggie's paws on the path.

My attention is caught by an early cluster of violets growing in the leaf mould. I slow and take a longer look at that leaf mould.

I've often thought about the fact that millions of deciduous trees across the length and breadth of the United Kingdom shed their leaves every autumn and winter. This rain of organic material, which then rots down to its particular constituents, must, over the centuries and millennia, have helped shape the landscape, providing essential elements of the soil that nurtures successive generations of plants.

Leaf mould is the most humble of substances. Lean down from your mobility scooter and scoop up a handful. Some would dismiss this as dirt. I regard it as the almost infinitely complex product of generations of living matter, layered by the season, marinated in rain, broken down by the processes of decomposition and metamorphosis, making its molecules available for growth and regeneration.

The closer you look at leaf mould, the more miraculous it seems, teeming with microbial life, worlds within worlds. Added to vegetable and flower beds, it boosts growth, provides pockets of air to otherwise dense soil, and feeds the inhabitants of the bed a wide variety of trace elements. Left on the ground where it formed, it helps the world remake itself season by season.

The experiences and memories we accumulate over time are not unlike leaf mould. Year by year, just as the leaves of a million trees rain down upon the ground, so an infinite number of sensory impressions – all those sounds! all those smells! – form strata of unremembered memories within us, from which, unconsciously, we draw inspiration for, among many other things, our writing.

Our subconscious mind acts as fertile ground in which memories ferment. They might be forgotten in our conscious waking life, yet they subtly influence our thoughts, feelings, and behaviours. Like the nutrients released by leaf mould, the essence of these buried memories seeps into our present reality and transforms it.

Sometimes, just as a knot of violets might unexpectedly sprout through leaf mould, a forgotten memory can resurface with startling clarity. A scent, a great tit's shrill cry, a familiar place – these can all act as triggers, unearthing fragments of our past. These unexpected resurgences illuminate the ongoing, dynamic interplay between the visible and invisible layers of our consciousness.

Our walk home that crisp morning, by some reckoning the first day of spring, provided me with another shower of memory leaves. By paying attention I was able to identify just some of the impressions that went to make up that sensory stratum. But whether or not you're focused on the sounds and smells and other sensations that you experience, the process is at work, moulding and remoulding the bedrock of your world.

WALKING ON WATER

We thought we'd escaped the worst effects of the latest cold spell to grip this sceptered isle. In December, ten days of sub-zero temperatures left the lake on which our houseboat floats frozen. Worse, from the perspective of the residents of Pontoon F the icy temperatures froze the pipes supplying us with clean water, and the pipes disposing of our waste water. "Keep calm and carry on," we muttered as we passed each other on the pontoon.

That was December. Now, in January, a second spell of unusually cold weather was forecast by the Met. Quite fortuitously, we'd arranged to spend a few days in the Lake District with a friend, and a couple more in Stow-on-the-Wold in the Cotswolds making arrangements for our writing weekend later in the year, so we imagined that by the time we got back to our lake the ice would have melted and the pipes thawed.

And so it seemed. We unlocked the gate that prevents curious passers-by from venturing onto the pontoon, and made our way down the causeway in the light drizzle that had greeted our return to Bedford.

The ice covering the lake indeed seemed to have melted. But

then we were struck by the sight of two of our resident swans just a few metres off the pontoon.

They were, to our astonishment, *standing* on the water.

"It's impossible," I muttered.

And then we realised it was just an illusion. The drizzle had covered the ice with a thin sheen of water. The swan was, indeed, standing on ice – but the ice was covered with a skim of water.

But for that moment, it had seemed like... magic.

Back in the late '70s, Peter Sellers starred in an extraordinary film called *Being There*. I'm not going to paraphrase the story – it's not necessary for my purposes here – but the film ends with the protagonist, a simple-minded man called Chancy Gardener, walking out onto a lake. He seems to be walking on water. But that image, like the image of our swans, is an illusion created artfully by the director as a means of underscoring the satirical message of his film.

Neither art nor artifice was involved in the illusion that so captivated us on Pontoon F. And yet it struck me that this is what all writers seek: the illusion of real life, of a real world in which real people make real choices. Fiction only works when the illusion is complete, when the swan – or Chancy Gardener – actually walks on water.

But when it works, we marvel: it's magical.

Which is perhaps why Colm Tóibín chose to call his book about Thomas Mann *The Magician**. Because he magicked worlds and characters into being. And because his simulacra were seamlessly convincing. The sheen of art concealed the artifice, the craft, the magician's tricks, that writers use to persuade readers of the reality of their fictions.

Three days after our return to our houseboat, the ice has melted, the swans glide imperiously across the lake, the magic, for the moment, has faded.

But it will return, I have no doubt.

. . .

* Mann's children called their father "the magician" because he performed magic tricks for them as children. But the nickname stuck.

GOOSEY, GOOSEY GANDER

The first sign we were given that a torrid spring lay ahead of us was Brenda's cry of dismay. "Get away," we heard, "go on, let me through!" Which was followed by a squeak and a muted but desperate "Help."

We found her standing on the pontoon confronted by an aggressive Canada goose, its wings half raised, its neck outstretched, its mouth open, hissing. Behind the goose, on the patch of astroturf that Brenda – one of our neighbours on Pontoon F – has fixed to the triangle at the back of her houseboat, stood another goose, and beside it, amidst a few scraps of weed, lay a large egg.

The drama of the situation was apparent at a glance.

Now, let me contextualise this scene. Our aquatic community consists of twelve houseboats arranged in herringbone fashion along a pontoon that stretches some fifty metres or so into our lake. We're situated in the last houseboat on the right. Brenda's is the second last on the left. Due to the geometry of herringbones, behind each houseboat there is a small triangle on which, variously, we've erected sheds, laid out pot plants or, in Brenda's case, created an intricate tapestry of garden ornaments and adornments. A bench took pride of place against the back wall of the houseboat. Arranged around it on the wall was a confection of masks: the Green Man alongside images of Father Thames and Poseidon. Porcelain lizards slithered up the wall. A small ladder was artfully placed on one side of the bench and a number of pot plants, together with two or three wooden birds – one a lugubrious duck – were balanced on its steps. Larger pot plants, including a luxuriant fern, were dotted around the astroturf.

You get the picture.

But now the sole and territorial occupant of this patch of fantastical conceits was a mother goose – a dame is what she should properly be called – with an egg. And according to English regulations, a nesting bird may not be disturbed.

The residents at the end of the pontoon learned how to deal with the goose's angry husband, the gander – they mate for life, by the way, and the ganders are fiercely protective of their dames during the brooding period. Whenever Trish passed by, for instance, she held an open umbrella out to confound the drake. Brenda armed herself with a broom.

And day by day, the dame added another egg to her clutch until she was the proud possessor of eight. She and her mate also added material to their nest drawn from underwater, from the banks of the lake, and from Brenda's various pot plants. In fact, the geese pretty quickly vandalised Brenda's garden, ripping the plants to shreds, incorporating one of the wooden ducks into their nest as a kind of bulwark, and so on. A visible component of the nest was the fern that every passer-by had once admired.

It was very distressing to Brenda.

We caught the occasional glimpse of the eggs when the dame took short breaks from her maternal duties. Her mate took to patrolling the waters on either side of the pontoon when he realised (this, of course, is an assumption, because it's difficult penetrating the mind of a goose) that we presented less of a threat to his potential offspring than other male geese in the vicinity did.

Several pitched battles took place between our gander and goosey rivals in the environs of Pontoon F.

We all looked up the gestation period of a Canada goose. Twenty eight days, we learned would pass between the laying of the last egg of the clutch and the hatching of all.* The first egg was laid on March 24. That meant that 36 days later, on April 29 or 30, the eggs would hatch, the adult geese would shepherd their family into the water, and the occupation would be over.

April 29 arrived. And passed. April 30 dawned. This must be the day, we decided. I took peeks at the nest several times over the course of the day.

No sign of the goslings.

May 1, 2 and 3 came and went. Deep misgivings took root in many of us.

"I'm not sure that these eggs are viable," I remarked gravely to Trish. "You give up hope too quickly," she said.

May 4, 5 and 6 passed. Our gander was growing impatient. He joined his mate on the pontoon. I imagined the two of them anxiously examining their clutch. But she continued to spend most of her days on her eggs.

The unseasonal cold of April gave way to a week of warmer weather. The goose spent more time off her nest.

"You see," Trish said, "she's letting the sun do her work for her. Clever goose."

But in our hearts we all knew that this was not the year in which these two geese would celebrate the birth of a fine clutch of offspring.

And yet nevertheless, our dame persisted for a few more days.

But by the end of another week, even she had to admit defeat. She abandoned the brood. The eggs, mottled and flaking, lay forlornly in the tatters of the nest.

I suspect that the pangs of grief that Canada geese feel under circumstances like this do not last long. And since they live for somewhere between ten and twenty-five years, there will be many more opportunities for procreation in the future.

And the relevance to us of their ordeal?

Well, the parallels seem obvious to me. I have for some weeks now been busy helping a writer develop an idea for a television series. We'd been struggling with the motivation of the antagonist. Why, precisely, did he take against our hero? Our initial assumptions didn't provide the kind of powerful motivation that our story demanded.

I cobbled together a *sort of* satisfactory storyline. But my last thought at night, as I brooded on our ideas, was that there was something wrong with our predicates.

And then yesterday I realised, with a start, that I was a goose trying to incubate a clutch of eggs that were unlikely ever to hatch. I had to begin again.

So I threw out our central idea, and played out in my mind a possible alternative.

And, by god, it worked.

We can pursue weak ideas for too long, convinced that there's a fix, a band-aid that'll somehow solve our plot problems. Often we're wrong. The only solution is to abandon the nest and find a radical alternative.

* Evolution has devised a nifty way of ensuring that all the goslings hatch more or less simultaneously. The dame will lay the entire clutch before beginning to incubate them, thus delaying the development of the foetal goslings until the starter's whistle sounds.

ADRIFT IN THE ELIZABETH WARD, BEDFORD HOSPITAL

Midway through 2022, I was holed up in a ward in Bedford Hospital for a little short of two weeks with a bad case of cellulitis. On one of her visits, Trish told me that the ward was reserved for the elderly and demented.

"Elderly? Am I elderly?" I asked, a note of defensiveness apparent even to me in my voice.

"Well," she said, "to be honest, you probably qualify."

"I don't *feel* elderly," I muttered. And I was pretty sure I wasn't demented – but then, perhaps, just as bores are never aware they're being boring, perhaps dementia has ambushed me while I wasn't watching.

Adrift, with a cannula pulsing at my wrist, and bag after bag of liquid antibiotics gravitating into my vascular system, I didn't feel much like writing.

But while I couldn't write, I could observe the incidents that on a daily basis entertained, amused or moved me – and make surreptitious notes of my observations.

What emerged from my stay in the Elizabeth Ward was a short series of hospital vignettes which I've collected here, as a demonstration of the value of keeping a notebook handy for precisely the sorts of experiences that might otherwise dissipate in the murky stream of memory.

The stories began in A&E before my admission.

1. Blood and laughter

She's loud, she could very well have had a drink or two too many - and there seems to be nothing the matter with her. Which is puzzling, since we're both in A&E at Bedford Hospital, along with thirty or forty others, some of them in a very bad way.

Let's clear up what I was doing there. On the way to hospital in the ambulance, a burly paramedic casually informed me that my symptoms were those of someone suffering an attack of cellulitis. Before I had time to interrogate him, we arrived, I was bundled out into a wheelchair, and wheeled up into the waiting room.

My right foot is now perched on a chair. It's swollen and red. I am waiting to be called through for a proper diagnosis and, hopefully, a cure.

Two seats along from me sits this loose-limbed, generously proportioned woman. She is very obviously not English. I know this not only because of her accent, which is vaguely Middle-Eastern, but because her first question to me is direct and to the point. "What's wrong with your leg?"

"They say, cellulitis."

"What is cellulitis?"

I shrug. I want to know, too. But, grateful to her for having broken the ice, I return the compliment. "And what's wrong with you?"

"Anxiety and depression," she offers, demonstrating not a whit of either in tone or manner. And then, with a toss of her head, and without further prompting, adds, "I wanted to commit suicide."

I'm not sure how to respond to this cheerful announcement. "I'm sorry," I say but she doesn't hear me because someone else on her left has caught her attention. It's a man with a very bloody knee. He's wearing on it a bandage that has not very successfully staunched the flow of blood, and on his face a very devilish grin.

"What was that?" she says sharply.

He leans forward. "Where do you live? Where's your place?"

"Two blocks away," she says. "Why do you ask?"

"I'm thinking," he says slyly, "that we could go there..."

"You and me?" She's astonished – and so am I, impressed by the directness of this Lothario's approach. I wonder what her riposte will be. She seems a no-nonsense kind of woman, who won't stand for cheek of any sort. But then her bosom shakes, she puts her head back, and she shrieks with laughter.

"We could go there now..." he repeats seductively.

"With your broken knee?" she splutters. "I wanted to commit suicide, and now look at me. I can't stop laughing." She smacks a prodigious thigh with the flat of her hand and breaks into more peals of laughter.

A nurse approaches briskly. "The doctor will see you now," she says, taking hold of my wheelchair and whisking me away. The joyous sound of whole-hearted laughter is cut off abruptly as the doors into the engine room of A&E swing shut behind us.

2. Where am I?

The patient in the bed nearest the bathroom is, of course, old. He's also confused.

"Where," he asks in a north country accent, "am I?"

The nurse at his bedside, sorting out his medication in a minute paper cup, says automatically: "You're in hospital, love."

He responds with some astonishment. "Hospital? Don't talk nonsense. I'm not in hospital. Why would I be in hospital?"

"You fell. The ambulance brought you in yesterday," she says patiently. This is not the first time she's answered these questions.

"I fell?!" he says incredulously. "I did not fall."

"Oh, yes, you did," she repeats.

The old man has extensive bruising on his shoulders and arm

– bruises that are exposed whenever the nurses give him a bed bath.

"I'm not in hospital," he declares again. Across the aisle running down the centre of the ward, another patient, my neighbour, a man who spends twelve or fourteen hours a day watching television and who's heard this interchange a dozen times and more over the past few days, calls out:

"Where do you think you are, then, Malcolm?" There's a note of derision in his voice.

We know his name is Malcolm because it's written on the large board above his bed. Malcolm Lowry. All our names are scrawled on similar boards above each of our beds.

Malcolm ponders this question for a few moments, frowning. "I'm on holiday," he says at last. He beams at the nurse who hands him the tiny paper cup with his pills. He gestures grandly at the ward and its occupants. "This is a holiday home."

"No, it's not," says the nurse, "you're in hospital."

Malcolm subsides, mumbling crossly to himself. "Hospital? Hospital? Why would I be in hospital."

For a moment there's comparative silence in the ward but for the murmur from my neighbour's television set. Then Malcolm's eye happens to catch his name on the board above him.

"Who wrote my name there?" he demands. This time I intervene.

"We all have our names above our beds, Malcolm. Have a look." He ignores me. He's still squinting at his own name.

"How do they know what my name is?" he asks indignantly.

"Don't worry about it," my neighbour tells him.

"Here's a glass of water, Malcolm," says the nurse. "Take your pills now, love."

He examines the contents of his little cup suspiciously, then up at the nurse standing at his bedside, his eyes wide, a little fearful.

"Where am I?" he says.

It's a good question, and one worth repeating. It's one that I guess we don't ask often enough. The answer, to some, is obvious: you're in hospital; you're at home; you're on a train.

But perhaps reality's more complex than that, requiring a more thoughtful answer. Perhaps we're the victims of a vast conspiracy, designed to hide the horrible reality of our situations from us, like Truman in *The Truman Show*. How *do* they know our names? And what are those pills they insist we swallow?

Perhaps paranoia is not just for the demented.

3. The colonel finds his teeth

The curtains are drawn around the corner bed diagonally opposite me in our ward, and have been for some time. Now a plaintive cry arises from the occupant, an elderly gent with a military bearing called Humphrey Grainger. I think of him as the colonel.

"Nurse, nurse," he cries out, his parade ground voice grown a little feeble with age, "the button isn't working."

I assume he means the button that dangles from a cord at the head of each bed that, pressed, summons assistance.

When his complaint is not answered, he sharpens his call. "The button that opens the curtain," he specifies. "It isn't working."

Now, this is strange since the only way to draw the curtains, thanks to a defect in their design, is to wrestle them along their runners. I've seen large male nurses struggle for minutes on end to draw or undraw them.

A nurse arrives.

"There isn't a button to open the curtains," she says, and begins manually yanking the curtain open to reveal the colonel within, sitting fully dressed on the side of his bed.

Watching her exertions, the colonel ponders this intelligence of a few moments. But then something more urgent than the curtains strikes him.

"Nurse, I wonder whether you could help me with a rather embarrassing issue." The colonel is unfailingly polite.

"What is it, darling?" Nurses routinely use the most intimate expressions of endearment to address us. I've never been as darling-ed and lovey-ed as I've been here, on the Elizabeth Ward.

He lowers his voice a little. "It's my teeth," he says. "I've looked everywhere for them. They seem to have disappeared."

"Your teeth."

The colonel is fretting, a touch querulous. "I had them at breakfast, but there's no sign of them now."

The nurse checks his locker-top.

"I've looked everywhere," he wails.

She turns to him and her mouth twitches. "Mr Grainger," she says. "Your teeth are in your mouth."

"In my mouth?" He claps a hand to his mouth. "Oh, my goodness, so they are. I am so dreadfully, dreadfully sorry."

"Not to worry, darling," she says. "I'm pleased we found them."

A LUTA CONTINUA

War talk is much in the air these days. We talk of "the war" in the way that our parents and grandparents must have referred, in their day, to "the war". We've learned or relearned the vocabulary of war. We've come to understand the difference between offensive and defensive tactics.

I've been engaged in a war of my own for three years now. It's a war not against a neighbouring territory – but there's no question at all that we've been invaded, and that in order to maintain our hold on what's ours, I've had to resort to both cunning and violence.

Three years ago Trish and I applied for an allotment. We were told that it would take at least two years for our name to rise to the top of the list. In the event, however, just a few months later a man from the council phoned and told us we were in luck. We arranged to meet at the allotment – just a fifteen-minute walk from our marina home – to inspect our new domain.

It was lovely. That is to say, it was covered in ash where the council had thoughtfully burnt the remnants of the previous occupant's shed, and hundreds of walnut shells, relics of a once enormous walnut tree that had stood on the allotment, disrespectfully casting deep shade over the adjoining plots. That, too, the council had disposed of.

There was also a fox hole. "You'll see it prowling around," our guide from a council, a little man with a small moustache and an air of great insouciance, said.

"And then, of course," he added ominously, "there's the bramble. Bugger to get rid of. Not sure I'd recommend you take this plot. Best wait for something easier."

But we were delighted with our allotment, bramble, fox hole and all, and signed on the dotted line. Annual rent: £35.

The bramble, though, *was* a bugger. It emerged from the ground in a great tangle of thorned vines. Some of these dived back into the ground to emerge at a little distance as new and even more vigorous secondary growths.

Initially I decided to tackle the Bramble Problem in our second year – but the sheer effrontery of the plant in invading our turf and blocking access to at least a third of the ground available to us finally decided me: "I'm going after the bramble," I told Trish grimly one day. "It's war."

I didn't bother with diplomatic protocol, just took a garden saw and a pair of powerful secateurs to it and over the course of several weekends reduced it to a heap of dismembered vines.

We celebrated my victory with a modest glass or two. The invasion had been repelled. Our territory was our own again.

Our first serious writing efforts are not unlike our allotment when we first clapped eyes on it. It is distinguished most by the ugly excrescences that mar it. Holes in our plots. Inelegancies in our writing. But because we are serious about mastering our craft, we correct what we can, perhaps take a writing class to gain the essential skills, and take an editing pencil, or its digital equivalent, to the most egregious faults in our text.

By the end of this process, we are more or less happy with

what we've written. We're ready for the next project to which we will apply all our newly learned skills. This one will be, if not perfect, then at least a damn sight better than the first.

In our second year on the allotment the enemy launched a retaliatory strike. It infiltrated terrain on which we'd already established spring crops of leeks and potatoes, strawberries and tomatoes, working its way underground and emerging at a number of different spots simultaneously, like those First World War spelunkers who drove tunnels under no man's land in order to attack enemy trenches from below.

No problem. I didn't need the saw this time, since all the emergent growth was fresh and comparatively thin. I counter-attacked with secateurs and after an afternoon of skirmishes, retired triumphant, albeit with arms scored and bleeding from the engagement.

I forget why, but for a couple of weeks we had to leave Bedford. On our return, I discovered that the enemy had taken advantage of our absence. Bramble stems arched high over the rhubarb. Some of the vines were thicker than my thumb. "In two weeks," I muttered. "Bloody hell."

All through that summer and autumn I waged relentless battle against the regiments of bramble that marched across the allotment, but by the end of autumn I again believed that I had vanquished the foe.

You return, refreshed to your computer, or your writing pad. You rattle off a page or two. That was easy, you think. I'm really getting the hang of it now.

You complete the story – or the first chapter of what you know is going to be a great novel. It's time for that celebratory drink. But before you crack the bottle of Dom, you have a second look at the immortal prose you've written.

You can't believe your eyes. Somehow, you've managed to write scenes that lack a dramatic imperative, the dialogue doesn't crackle, and as for the cliffhangers – well, the question is, *what* cliffhangers? There's no suspense! Ohmigod. These are lessons drummed into you during the course you enrolled on. They were in your head – but somehow they didn't make it onto the page.

Clearly, mastering this writing business is not as simple as it seems.

We were ready for them in year three, but even so we were surprised by the speed of their initial attack. Again, tendrils of bramble poked their heads up above ground across half the allotment.

But I was ready and guillotined them with enthusiasm.

We're in mid-summer now, but I know that, although they'll keep coming, they lack the energy – and the weaponry – that they exhibited on their earlier incursions.

Incorporating new skills into your arsenal is not an overnight affair. It takes time. And even after you've mastered all the skills, you'll still find the odd weed poking its head up in your prose. But over time, fewer of these appear – and it becomes easier and easier to lop off their heads.

So although the war is never over, with time, you'll find it easier and easier to send the rascals, when they do have the audacity to return, packing.

5

THE RIVER GREAT OUSE

AND OTHER SEAS

THREE PERSPECTIVES

Chugging along a river or canal in a narrowboat gives you a certain perspective on... life, I suppose, but more immediately, your specific and ever-changing environment. At three or four miles per hour, it's not altogether astonishing that you notice details – the wildflowers, about which I've written before – the trees, the shadowed bowers in the woods, the glimpse, in spring, of clearings bursting with undulating carpets of bluebells.

You have time, as you sip your mug of coffee, your hand lightly resting on the tiller, the diesel engine beneath your feet humming throatily, to cast your eyes up, following a raucous crow on its untidy flight to a branch in one of a line of towering poplars... Or you note on a distant hill the chalk lion of, ah, it must be Whipsnade Zoo. Or, ahead of you on the canal, the cascade erupting between ancient wooden lock gates.

You congratulate yourself a little smugly on your wisdom at having abandoned the highways of this world for your placid, waterborne existence. You reflect how much you miss of the wonders of the everyday when you're hurtling along the M1 at 80 miles an hour.

But then, later, having settled on a new permanent mooring

on a lake surrounded by trees that gesticulate wildly in any wind, you buy a kayak and venture out onto waters made familiar by your frequent narrowboat sorties. You paddle a mile upriver to the Town Lock, and a mile downriver to Cardington Lock – and you're astonished by what fresh wonders you behold:

A mallard mother anxious over her newly-hatched brood of twelve chicks that whizz around her like rocket-propelled scraps of fluff;

A pair of swans jealously guarding their clutch on a nest tucked away between a reed bed and a public footpath, hidden from passing walkers by a screen of hawthorn;

A heron, standing solitary guard on a willow branch protruding horizontally from the tree's gnarled trunk. It gazes intently at the water beneath it. You stop paddling and allow your kayak to drift silently towards the skittish bird. You dare not breathe for fear of putting the heron to flight. Fifteen yards, twelve yards, ten. You're as close as you've been to one of the giant inhabitants of the riverways. And then something alerts it, and its narrow head turns and one eye squints at you, alarmed, and then its wings come up and it pulls itself into the air, like an unfurling umbrella, and, rising, turns and lifts away with a rasping eldritch cry.

Later still, when the long-delayed summer at last arrives, you risk a toe in the murky water of the river and think of dipping into its coolth. You abandon both narrowboat and kayak and slip into the lake and make your way through banks of waterweed to the river beyond.

Now you're at water level. What took one minute in the narrowboat and five minutes in the kayak, takes twenty minutes in the water. Your body is alive to every underwater swirl of the river. You're aware of the dust of pollen on the surface. A pair of Egyptian geese swim regally by, unperturbed by these novel water creatures in their midst. A kingfisher flashes past just above your head.

You're not looking at the river now – you're immersed in it.

It all depends on your perspective. Change it, and a new world comes into view.

And later, when you're towelling yourself dry, a further thought occurs to you. Just as different levels of immersion afford you different perspectives, and different perspectives expose you to different experiences of the world, so you can, as a writer, choose which level at which to explore your reader's experience of the world of your story.

You want him to enjoy a God's-eye view of events? Then adopt the perspective of the all-knowing author who knows everything and can tantalise the reader with hints of what's afoot behind the arras or in the future.

You want to give your reader a flavour of your character's more intimate experience of the world? Then choose to tell it from her perspective, giving us a flavour of her ever-changing moods or the finely granulated nature of her moral sensibilities.

And if you want to plunge into the very waters of her experience, then you can choose a perspective that reports on the flood of sensations coursing through her consciousness – as Joyce did in that exultant stream of consciousness that takes us to the core of Molly Bloom's experience of being... Molly Bloom.

A HABIT OF WRITING

After a long break, Trish and I have taken to the River Great Ouse again on our kayak. In summer, we'd venture out onto the river four or five days a week, paddling our way up as far as the town lock, or downstream to Cardington Lock. It's a mile each way, so these journeys – as the pike swims at any rate – demand two miles of paddling. But because we nose into one or other bank of the river in our explorations, and occasionally double back on ourselves, I reckon we're entitled to notch up more than that.

That's not what it's about, of course. I've alluded before to the calming effects of immersing yourself totally in the natural world. And whether we're swimming, in the river, kayaking on it, or charging along it in our narrowboat, Patience, at three miles an hour, we're aware of being clasped in nature's bosom.

But it is also excellent exercise. A one-hour paddle leaves you pleasantly aware of the fact that locomotion takes effort, and effort stretches and works muscles in parts of your body of which you are otherwise only peripherally aware.

So why did we stop for at least two months? Ah, well, life is full of surprises. The first surprise was the minor op I had to remove a couple of benign lipomas from my back. The procedure went well, but it took some weeks for the wounds to heal and during this period I was advised not to challenge my back muscles with any strenuous exercise.

And then there was the tear in the fabric of the kayak. It's an inflatable, so a tear is potentially catastrophic. It took us some time to repair it.

And then... we just fell out of the habit. That's the key to this story. We knew kayaking was the source of deep pleasure. We knew it constitutes excellent exercise, but if you break the habit, these arguments to resume the habit lose traction.

But yesterday, with the temperature hovering at just 2 or 3 degrees Celsius, Trish inflated the kayak, launched it and we took our customary places in it – Trish in the bow, me in the stern. And we paddled downstream, stopping in the empty lock at Cardington for tea (Trish) and coffee (me). Powered boats don't use the river much in winter, so we were reasonably sure we wouldn't be told to move.

Having tea or coffee is part of the habit, you see – although sometimes, after we've been very good, we reward ourselves with a flask of whisky and, at the end of a long summer's day, take refuge from the sun beneath the foliage of a particular horse chestnut that spreads its boughs generously across the water.

That's my subject today, if you hadn't guessed: habits.

They're all the rage. One of the best-selling non-fiction books of the century is called *Atomic Habits* by James Clear (great name for a writer) in which he anatomises habits, and prescribes how to develop the sorts of habits that further our goals.

The thing is, we're fully aware that writing something clearly and elegantly brings a rare sense of satisfaction. We know that creating a complex character, or pulling off a complex scene, is deeply fulfilling. We know that writing creatively is, in itself, therapeutic.

And yet sometimes life gets in the way, and we can realise with a start that we haven't pounded the keys for weeks... months... even longer.

There's only one way to solve this, people. However inept you feel, however unexercised those writing muscles are, however unqualified your inner critic insists you are, you must pick up the pen, or open the laptop and start.

A paragraph is not an insurmountable obstacle. A page can appear on your screen before you're aware of it. Of course, it doesn't take just one session to re-establish the habit. Experience tells me that it takes a week to weave writing back into your life.

Which is why, in just an hour or two, Trish and I plan to slip back into the kayak and head off, this time, for the town lock. Yesterday we retrieved two glittering fishing lures from the bare branches of willow trees, abandoned by frustrated fishermen on the opposite bank.

Who knows, today we might find even more exotic treasures.

FOUR LITTLE DUCKS PADDLING DOWN THE OUSE

Let's begin with a detail – and then broaden our focus until we take in every inquiry you've ever launched.

The detail is a glimpse of yellow on the river, caught between two half-submerged willow branches that effectively cut off navigation around one side of a small island upstream from our marina.

Trish and I spend hours collecting debris from the River Great Ouse: beer cans, gin bottles, take-away cartons, sodden plastic bags. On this occasion – for reasons that'll become clear in a minute – I was not scooping up rubbish, and nor was Trish with me. But that bright gleam of yellow was enticing. What, I wondered, could it be?

I manoeuvred the kayak and thrust my way between obstructing branches until I was near enough to dip my paddle in the water under the object of my curiosity and raise it up for closer inspection. It was, of course, more than probably just a half-submerged can of some vile sweet drink.

But no. I felt my mouth widen in a smile of delight. What was balancing precariously on the curve of my paddle was a small rubber duck, clearly launched by a child and lost to the racing current.

And then, probably because my eye was now keyed to the shape of the little duck, I picked out in the cleft between the branches another duck. This one was blue. And alongside it, bobbing bravely, a third, a green duck.

There you go. If you follow the impulse of curiosity, who knows what you'll find. This is as true on the river as off it. It is as true in life, as it is in writing. Writers are curious about the world and all the things and people in it. In seeking to satisfy their curiosity they invent scenarios, possibilities, that emerge from the questions they have asked. I have spent an hour wondering about the children who must have launched their ducklings upon the rushing waters of the Ouse. I wonder what *they* imagined has become of them.

But folks, there's more: a chance discovery gives rise to questions. In this case I pondered the three ducks that I'd set up on the kayak before me. A yellow one, a green one and a blue one. Surely, somewhere, there must be a red duck?

So on my way back to the marina I let my eyes play curiously across the water, probing the shadows beneath overhanging banks, scanning the tangles of branches and twigs caught at choke points along the river.

And then, well, you've guessed it, of course. A red duck joined his fellows on the kayak.

Curiosity, discovery – sometimes unexpected, often delightful – followed by deduction, investigation, speculation, further discoveries... This is the chain of logic and inspiration that leads to creation.

Let's never forget that the natural curiosity we were born with is one of those gifts that we should always treasure – and exercise as often as possible.

Oh, by the way, let me satisfy whatever residual curiosity you have about my reason for not scouring the river for rubbish on this particular voyage. On a recent recce in Venice to identify a new fabulous venue for our writing retreats, a great storm lashed the British Isles. Gale force winds battered the marina – and took with them our inflatable kayak.

Of course, we mourned its loss – but we so love our time on the river that we didn't delay in ordering a replacement: a solid plastic two-and-a-half-person vessel, red as that final duckling. And I was making my first, my maiden voyage in the new kayak, when I encountered the ducks, and the subject for this piece.

BUTTONS AND HYPODERMIC NEEDLES

Between trips on the river in our spanking new kayak, and dips in its waters on our regular wild swimming expeditions, I've been reading Colm Tóibín's *The Magician.* It's a biographical novel which takes as its subject the life of one of the twentieth century's most revered writers, the German Thomas Mann.

On Page 382 Tóibín has Mann say this:

> Yes, it is a grubby business writing novels. Composers can think about God and the ineffable. We have to imagine the buttons on a coat.

It's a wonderful thought to give a man renowned for the realism of his novels, and it pierces to the heart of the narrative project. Because how *do* you, as a writer, create on the page, the simulacrum of reality? By tackling grand themes? By developing your talent for lyricism?

Or by learning from Jane Austen the virtues and the value of taking detailed and meticulous notes on what she called her "little bit of ivory" – a pocket diary that she carried with her in which she recorded her observations of people and their peculiarities, and then having them serve your dramatic purpose: which is to create a world into which your readers can sink.

Because it is the buttons that convince, not the grand conceptual gestures. What, in a different context, Yeats called "the foul rag and bone shop of the heart".

Get the details right – the buttons and the eyebrows, the unique quirks of a character's speech, the meerschaum pipe, the seven percent solution of cocaine – and the big ideas will take care of themselves.

This *is* a big idea, that Tóibín expressed perfectly, through his character's mouth, in just three sentences. What more need be said?

In case you missed the reference, the "seven per cent solution" refers to Sherlock Holme's addiction to cocaine. We were introduced to it on the opening page of Conan Doyle's *The Sign of the Four*, first published in book form in 1890. Here's the opening paragraph, and a couple more, which, though they contain no buttons, are replete with specific and altogether convincing detail:

> Sherlock Holmes took his bottle from the corner of the mantelpiece and his hypodermic syringe from its neat morocco case. With his long, white, nervous fingers he adjusted the delicate needle, and rolled back his left shirt-cuff. For some little time his eyes rested thoughtfully upon the sinewy forearm and wrist all dotted and scarred with innumerable puncture-marks. Finally he thrust the sharp point home, pressed down the tiny piston, and sank back into the velvet-lined arm-chair with a long sigh of satisfaction...
>
> "Which is it to-day?" I asked, – "morphine or cocaine?"
>
> He raised his eyes languidly from the old black-letter volume which he had opened. "It is cocaine," he said, "a seven-per-cent. solution. Would you care to try it?"

Plots are two a penny. Anyone can think up a half-way decent plot if they set their minds to it. But it's the details that distinguish the best stories, honest, accurate, specific details.

We live, as you know, on a lake that adjoins a river. It's only when I paint the specific details of our location – the blue flash of a kingfisher, the dimpled tug of water round a willow branch, the dusting of pollen on the surface of the river – that it all comes into focus.

WHERE BOUNDARIES DISSOLVE

I'm not sure where this is going to lead me today, but I'm going to take a chance and risk writing something that might end up going nowhere useful at all.

Bear with me.

Let's start with the idea of boundaries. A few weeks ago I started thinking about boundaries and what they signify. Perhaps this had something to do with the war in Ukraine – and the fact that Russia refuses to acknowledge the primacy of the boundaries that demarcate its territory...

Or it could be that recently we spotted a species of duck we'd never seen before on Longholme Lake, which sits, curiously, between two branches of the River Great Ouse. It was a handsome bird which we learned is called a scaup... Britain's rarest breeding duck. (Or, it could be it was the rather more common tufted duck: they look remarkably similar. We opted for the scaup.)

Now any given species – whether avian or any other – is defined at least partly by the fact that it can't breed with any other species. There are, in other words, strict boundaries between species.

Except that... there aren't. Birds from closely related species do indeed breed, and produce hybrids which may or may not be capable of reproducing.

But surely some boundaries are impermeable? Boundaries like that between fiction and non-fiction; between the products of the imagination, and facts which are, I suppose, the products of the material world.

Or is this boundary as impenetrable as we assume? We've learned in the last few years that for some people at least there are facts... and then there are alternative facts. Many of us – most of us, I fervently hope – would call these "alternative facts" lies, or at least fabulations.

And yet, and yet... The fictions so many of us consume, and that some of us produce, are also the vehicles of truth – the essential truths that make life worth living. Truths that concern doubt and courage, love and fealty (among many other qualities).

So what am I saying? That the sort of boundaries we rely on for clarity are less reliable than we'd like? Or that every moral choice is much more complex than we'd hope it would be? Or that the boundary between good and evil is ambiguous at best?

Ambiguity in life is always slightly discombobulating. It means we can never be certain of another's motives; or of our own rectitude.

But in fiction, ambiguity is to be welcomed, since the shadows are always more interesting than the spotlight; and what goes on in the wings is so often more compelling than what's happening on the stage.

So when next you consider what separates good from bad, or cowardice from courage, or love from hate, remember that these contradictions are frequently only apparent and that, perhaps, writers interested in exploring the "truth" should concern themselves with this hybrid space, these interstices, where nothing is quite as we'd imagined.

THE BUTCHER OF ST NEOTS

St Neots, a small town straddling the River Great Ouse a few locks down from Bedford, holds a market every Thursday in the town square. It was the site, in July 1648, of a pitched battle between Royalists, supporters of Charles I, and Parliamentary troops, the Roundheads.

There's no sign of enmity between opposing factions today, although it's true that this section of Cambridgeshire bucked the trend established in the rest of the county and voted to leave the EU in the fateful Brexit referendum back in 2016.

After the enforced isolation of Covid, and a two-year hiatus during which we gutted our narrowboat Patience, and rebuilt it from the floor up, we were celebrating our return to the river with a week-long cruise.

Our first overnight stop was against the grassy bank of a small riverine island where we were surrounded, on the water, by flowering lilies, and on the island by a constant chorus of birdsong.

St Neots was our next stop. We crossed the bridge from our mooring on the far side of the river and made our way to the town square. Stalls had been erected selling everything from cheese to electric mobility scooters. Shoppers foraged among the shelves of a second-hand bookstore. Old men took the sun on benches, and customers crowded the tables of the Café Nero at one end of the square.

But the market was dominated by a large, refrigerated vehicle, custom-built to display a wide variety of cuts of meat.

In addition to various printed notices advertising rolled beef, rump steak, and so on, there were also hand-written signs featuring a series of idiosyncratically spelt offers: BUFFERLOW WINGS, for instance, were available at £20. SMOKEY JOE CHICKIN PORTIONS rubbed shoulders with another placard offering a BRECKFAST PACK containing LOTS OF GAMON STEAKS, A PACK OF BACON AND PORK SAUSAGE.

All of this, though, was merely the stage for the star of the show. The proprietor, a burly man in his forties, stood behind his counter high above the ground, dressed in a traditional striped butcher's apron, and wearing a mic connected to an effective public address system.

"Here we have the most delicious cut of sirloin, ladies and gents," he said with infectious enthusiasm. "I'm giving it away for just twenty pound." Then he lowered his voice and added, confidentially, "But for just thirty, I'll give you two. Now, you can't ask for better than that."

And on and on he went. "You, young lady, you look like a passable cook," he said, addressing a white-haired woman perched on a mobility scooter. "Close your eyes and imagine this on your dinner table..."

When we set out to write a story of some description – a short story, a novel, a memoir – we take great care to ensure that we have the meat and potatoes necessary to fashion a decent meal. We might imagine that that's enough to satisfy our readers.

The sirloin and chicken and pork that the butcher of St Neots had laid out on the counters in his refrigerated truck were, I'm sure, pretty standard fare. It took the magic of his performance to transform it into something truly desirable. He recognised that people enjoy being entertained, they love drama, they relish surprises. He was happy to take on the persona of a carnival barker to attract the crowds – and sell his goods.

And by the end of the day that is precisely what he'd done.

Of course the story you've devised is as solid as you can make it. But now you have to work out how to make the characters as memorable as possible, the twists and turns of the tale as unexpected as they are surprising. And you have to approach each scene with this thought in mind: how do I write this as entertainingly as I can?

P.S. Early landowners in St Neots – then known as Eynesbury – realised that in order to attract visitors to the local priory, (and spend their money at local hostelries) they needed a unique selling proposition. "If only," they mused, "we could somehow get our hands on the bones of a saint." Holy relics were all the rage in the eleventh and twelfth centuries. "We'd become the focus of pilgrimages," they reasoned. One of them had made a pilgrimage to St Neot in Cornwall, where the bones of the founding saint of that priory – a man noted for his piety and wisdom – were interred. They nicked his bones – leaving just an arm behind – and hot-footed it for Eynesbury. The bones were put on display, the word soon got out, and pilgrims flocked to the priory which became rich and famous as a result, and the town became known as St Neots. Another lively example of showmanship – and a little larceny – in action.

O MY! O MY! O MY!

Yes, of course literary conflict provides the driving impetus of all narrative. But from time to time every writer earns the right to indulge their desire simply to celebrate beauty or tranquillity.

We've just spent eight days cruising down our river, leaving Priory Marina in Bedford for the distant river port of St Ives, twenty nine miles, five and a quarter furlongs* downstream from us.

The weather was for the most part fine. Only one shower caught us unawares – but provided welcome relief from the mid-summer heat.

At every turn of the river – and there are many of them – we were greeted by prospects of great charm and beauty. Leaving each of the nine locks we passed through, we found ourselves plunged into a green world, the foliage so thick on either side of the river and overhead, that it brings to mind Andrew Marvel's wonderful line of "a green thought in a green shade".**

Another turn brings a line of towering poplars into view, over-topping a copse of oaks and horse chestnuts, the last remnants of their candelabra blossoms serving as nests for a crop of conkers.

And there to the left of us, along the bank, a field of flowering white lilies with their enticing bundles of yellow stamens...

Now, sitting at the tiller on the stern deck of a narrowboat slowly puttering along through mile after mile of great natural beauty has a deep effect on me. It calms me. It erases tension and anxiety. In the parlance of the moment, it is very good for my mental health.

But great mental health is not the subject of story. Story depends on fracture. On being thrown out of your comfort zone. On being confronted by problems and conundrums, puzzles and discord. Serenity is what sometimes lies at the end of the journey. If your protagonist is lucky, resolution takes place only after he has dealt with his demons and overcome his adversaries.

So what message for you, gentle reader, could I possibly derive from eight tranquil days on the water?

And that's when I decided not to seek discord where none exists, but to celebrate, for this moment at least, the uncomplicated natural world of the river and its environs.

Four days after we set off, I brought Patience gently up against the town quay in St Ives, slipping neatly into the last slot between a cruiser and a flight of stone steps leading up from the river. I turned off the engine, and with my companions tied up securely to the bollards above us.

And a passage occurred to me from Kenneth Grahame's *The Wind in the Willows.* It was drawn to my attention by a very useful website we use to plan our voyages. Every day they post a quotation that relates in one way or another to the endless pleasures of the waterways of the United Kingdom. Here it is:

> Leaving the main stream, they now passed into what seemed at first sight like a little land-locked lake. Green turf sloped down to either edge, brown snaky tree-roots gleamed below the surface of the quiet water, while ahead of them the silvery shoulder and foamy tumble of a weir, arm-in-arm with a restless dripping mill-wheel, that held up in its turn a grey-gabled mill-

house, filled the air with a soothing murmur of sound, dull and smothery, yet with little clear voices speaking up cheerfully out of it at intervals. It was so very beautiful that the Mole could only hold up both forepaws and gasp, 'O my! O my! O my!'

* That's 47 kilometres, more or less, in the decimal world. A furlong was originally defined as the distance a team of oxen could plough without resting.

** Here's the enigmatic stanza in which that line occurs:

Meanwhile the mind, from pleasure less,
Withdraws into its happiness;
The mind, that ocean where each kind
Does straight its own resemblance find,
Yet it creates, transcending these,
Far other worlds, and other seas;
Annihilating all that's made
To a green thought in a green shade.

THE HEROES OF THE SCILLY ISLES

Let me develop a scenario, beginning from what really happened and then invent elements that might turn it into a story, along the lines, you might have guessed from a preoccupation that has revealed itself in my previous musings, of the Hero's Journey.

The point of doing this is to explore what it takes to turn a series of relatively mundane incidents into a rollicking tale of a hapless adventurer and his companion – and, crucially, how using the scaffolding of the Hero's Journey can help with that construction.

Here's what happened:

Trish and I were on a brief holiday on the island of Tresco in the Scilly Isles, 40 miles or so south-west of Land's End in Cornwall. We brought with us our inflatable kayak in which over the past year or so we've been exploring the River Great Ouse. For the first five days of our stay we were prevented from launching it by a Force Eight Gale that lashed the islands.

But at last the wind relented and we inflated the kayak and set out from the beach at Old Grimsby Quay. A breeze was blowing, but the sun was shining, and we happily paddled along, hugging the coast past the Old Blockhouse (built in the sixteenth century) and on past a series of small bays, rounding Rushy Point and headed for Lizard Point. Across the channel from Tresco lay St Martins Island, one of the five inhabited islands of the Scillies. A scattering of other islands, some mere rocky outcrops, others more substantial, lay between us and St Martins.

At times we had to paddle into the small swells raised by the breeze, and at times we found ourselves running athwart the swells. At no point did we feel in any danger – although the reports I'd read about unfortunate canoeists losing their lives in these waters did sometimes pop unbidden into my head.

We considered briefly pushing on to the next big crescent beach – Pentle Bay – but then thought better of it, turned and paddled back up the coast to our point of embarkation. The entire "adventure" had taken perhaps an hour, and we'd travelled a mile or so down the coast before returning.

So, no great shakes. It was a delightful paddle – but hardly something one could call an epic adventure.

And yet...

The experience contained an embryonic Hero's Journey. Consider: Before the Hero begins his Journey, he lives in what's called The Ordinary World, the world he's familiar with, the world he knows. That's us, on the beach. We're familiar with river kayaking. We know our way about the Great Ouse.

But there before the Hero lies the challenge of an Adventure: the open ocean, the vast north Atlantic. It's unfamiliar territory. The conditions are unpredictable. (The wind could rise, those small swells could become rolling mountains of water.) The Hero has his doubts about his ability, and fears for his safety. (I remembered the stories of drowned innocents.)

But he sets aside his doubts and launches himself into the Special World of his Journey. We set off towards Blockhouse Point. As it happens, apart from a sense that these waters were very different from the waters of the Ouse ("It feels a lot livelier, doesn't it?" I asked Trish), we had no trouble in slicing through the wavelets.

But classically, the Hero encounters a series of tests and trials during this stage of the Journey. What might have happened to challenge us? Well, a whole number of things are possible. We might have been blown off course by a stiffening wind, ending up not at the mouth to Pentle Bay, but on one of the uninhabited islets in the channel between Tresco and St Martins.

Or we might have capsized and lost our paddles. We'd then have found ourselves at the mercy of both currents and winds that conceivably could have taken us out of the comparatively sheltered waters between the islands into the open ocean.

One possibility could have given rise to others. Each would have confronted us with a challenge that tested our mettle to the utmost (a stormy night on a fragment of rock; a night on the heaving main). We would have faced not simply the elements, but the stark possibility of our own deaths – an experience that in the Hero's Journey is called The Ordeal.

But of course we'd have survived, rescued perhaps by a passing yacht, or a boat of the Royal National Lifeboat Institution – or thanks to our own initiative.

And we'd have returned to our cottage on Tresco, chastened but invigorated by the knowledge that we'd survived everything fate and the ocean had thrown at us. That's the Boon the Hero gains from his experience.

Even the tamest paddle along the coast contains the seeds of a mighty adventure that could fill a book with compelling story.

And so it is with many of our everyday experiences that pass unnoticed and unremarked, but that could form the basis for richly imagined tales.

INTO THE CLEAR LIGHT OF DRAMATIC TRUTH

We're about to cruise past Torghatten, a mountain on an island a kilometre or two off the Norwegian mainland, and just half an hour south of the Arctic Circle. It's distinguished by an astonishing hole driven clear through it. Some 20m wide and 35m high, it is 160 m long. From a distance, when the weather permits, you can see right through it to the sky beyond.

Our little company of four, sitting in the starboard lounge of the *Spitsbergen,* en route for Bergen, speculated about the nature and the cause of the hole. One of us hypothecated that the action of water from a plateau beyond the mountain – a plateau now long eroded away, he suggested – had, over time, worked its way through a fault in the mountain.

Nonsense, said another one of us, why look for a complicated explanation when a simple one is at hand: google it.

So we did. And discovered a few explanations. The first was roughly what one of us had suggested: wind and ice had bored its patient way through a layer of softer rock, leaving in its wake the cathedral-sized hole.

See, crowed the proponent of erosion theory.

But there is a secondary explanation for the origin of Torghatten's hole.

According to one legend of these Helgeland mountains, Torghatten was formed when the troll, Hestmannen, disappointed in love, shot an arrow at a young and comely maiden called Lekamøya. The local Troll-King, enraged by this injustice, in an instant frisbeed his hat to intercept the arrow before it nailed the hapless Lekamøya. The arrow did, however, pierce the hat... And then the sun rose and everyone involved in this little piece of drama was turned to stone, including the hat, with a hole drilled neatly through its heart.

The question is, which explanation do you prefer? Obviously, the geological explanation is the true one – but it is a much less satisfactory story than the tale of Hestmannen, Lekamøya and the Troll-King.

Clearly, stories of trolls and virgin maidens are more romantic and more compelling than a prosaic explanation that involves the slow work of water and ice on less than obdurate rock.

But there's another reason the one is so much more appealing than the other, I think, and that is that the legend is full of the fire of love and rejection, of disappointment and pity. These are all emotionally charged motivations, different in kind from the dry cause-and-effect chain of events that links the elements of the geological story.

Stories that fail to yoke the emotions will fail, more or less; those that find and exploit the emotions at the heart of otherwise heartless events, will succeed.

And wherever there's a prosaic explanation for something, there's also likely to be another that's both more electric and more memorable. The first version that occurs to you might well be a little obvious, a little quotidian: water trickling over rock. Dig deeper, though, and you might well find your story piercing the mountain and emerging into the clear air of dramatic truth on the other side.

6

VENICE

THE BELLS OF VENICE

Every year Trish and I and our South African partner in All About Writing, Jo-Anne, decamp to Venice to hold a writing retreat for a dozen or more fellow writers. And since Venice is half land, half sea, it qualifies for inclusion in a book devoted to watery inspiration.

Venice is a city of bells. They ring out at unpredictable hours from church towers across the city. The loudest are the bells of the San Marco campanile, but every neighbourhood has its churches – there are 118 in all – and so the sound of bells is very much part of every visitor's experience.

Working in my hotel room in that part of the city called Dorsoduro a few days before the start of one writing retreat, I was woken by a nearby bell ringing melodiously. A few seconds later, another nearby bell started ringing.

The pace of the second bell was slightly faster than the first so that after a few seconds the two bells rang simultaneously, before the second overtook the first. And then gradually increased its lead until, in due course, it bumped up against the first...

I thought: how would I describe this fairly simple sensory experience? Of one bell ringing once every three seconds, and the second, once every two and a half seconds... The first, lower-voiced bell establishes the beat; the second, slightly higher in tone, weaves its way around the first...

And then I realised that, as a non-musician, I don't really have the vocabulary to write an accurate description... If I'd known what note each bell was sounding, I could have done something with that. If I'd known what the technical terms were for the phenomenon, I could have structured my description around them.

I wondered how I might have woven my description around one of my favourite words: tintinnabulation...

I remembered a friend who, years ago, and in secret, set out to write a science fiction novel. He wrote it – and, in fact, a sequel, and found a publisher for them. I'm not sure how well they did, whether the royalties were worth the effort, or whether he was tempted to write a third.

What I do remember very clearly is his telling me how he practised writing fight sequences in preparation for the novel. His story required that he write a number of action sequences. Since he had himself never in all his life found himself fighting another, he felt deeply unqualified to do so. So he practised. And practised. Trying to get the energy, the rhythm, the details right.

Why, indeed, should any of us be capable of recreating a complex situation – a fight, an argument, a dinner party, a children's party, two bells ringing on a Venetian afternoon – without practice? It seems absurd on the face of it.

So that's a challenge I'm giving myself: to write as precise a description as I can of those two bells ringing slightly out of sync. And to rewrite it as many times as I need until I've got as close to the experience as I can.

And perhaps then I'll turn to something really complex – like *three* bells ringing slightly out of sync...

A FRAGILE BARQUE UPON A SEA OF POSSIBILITY

Preparing for another writing retreat, I came across, as one is bound to, the notes Henry James made about the city of Venice... A line or two caught my attention. Here they are:

> But in truth, Venice isn't in fair weather a place for concentration of mind. The effort required for sitting down to a writing-table is heroic, and the brightest page of MS looks dull beside the brilliancy of your milieu. All nature beckons you forth and murmurs to you sophistically that such hours should be devoted to collecting impressions. Afterwards, in ugly places, at unprivileged times, you can convert your impressions into prose. Fortunately for the present proser the weather wasn't always fine...

If James is right, and he's not often wrong, then I hope that every morning we spend in the gilded city will have foul weather, and that the rest of every day and night be as brilliant as it may be.

But weather aside, and, indeed, Venice aside, Henry James brings up an issue about which writers can burble for hours at a time, and that is... Where do they do their best work?

At a table overlooking the Grand Canal? (James, Byron) At a window overlooking your garden? (P.G. Wodehouse) In a cubby hole without a view of any kind? (Stephen King) At night, when they're wrapped in shadows? (Dickens, Neruda, Frost, Proust) At the kitchen table surrounded by the bustle of everyday life? (E.B. White) In a hotel room from which all ornaments and decorations have been removed? (Maya Angelou). In a rented office with any means of connecting to the internet disabled? (Jonathan Franzen)

Matt Shoard reports in *The Guardian* that J.D. Salinger's "last unpublished work – written in slippers and robe in New Hampshire, and burned at dusk – was a song to insomnia, a 'memoir of the night' of which only 16 pages remain."

It's clear there is no ideal place or time to write. We each make our own. And if we're clever, we broaden the opportunities to write by not obsessively limiting ourselves to a single favourite place. I've written scripts on a Zanzibari island, on the Trans-Canadian express from Vancouver to Toronto, on our narrowboat, Patience, on the English canals (many of them, it must be said), in coffee shops from here to, well, not Kingdom Come, but a stop or two short of that...

But there surely has to be a quality common to all the places in which one feels free to indulge the urge to write. Something in the air – or the white noise! – that encourages you to relax your inhibitions. Something, too, that enables you to write unobserved, like a spider working patiently on a web in a high corner of the room. Anonymity is vitally important.

And above all, you must feel that *here* it is possible to launch the fragile barque of your imagination into the unknown seas that lie beneath the mists ahead.

THE POWER OF TEXTURAL MEMORY

Returning to Venice as we do every year reveals the power of textural memory. You might not remember what palazzo lies round the next corner of the Grand Canal – but you do remember the groaning of the rope as it brings the tethered vaporetto to a stop

You might not remember precisely the route from San Silvestro to the square in which your lodgings – a grand palazzo, time-stained and shabbily imperious – are to be found, but you do remember the texture of those unplastered walls, or the washing hanging from the lines three stories up, or that faint smell of stale sea water as you cross one of the canals on your way.

Textural memory is memory writ small. It's usually not labelled, nor does it come decorated with capitals. It's humble. It asks no favours. It seems undistinguished and unremarkable.

And yet it is the memory that lingers, so there's no question that we did, somehow, without knowing, remark it. It lies somewhere in the interstices of our brains waiting to snap back into life, vibrant as ever it was.

Writing that papers its walls with textural detail is, to nudge that metaphor another inch or two along, wraparound. It fills our senses. It stretches from horizon to sensory horizon. It's evocative. It triggers cascades of associations.

The bells are ringing in Venice again as I write this line. It's twelve o'clock on a Sunday, and a hundred towers resound with the clamour of brass and iron. I can't see any single bell from my vantage point – but I can hear them all, and together they constitute a three-dimensional soundscape that will live with me, I have no doubt, forever.

The canny writer calls on everyday textures to complete the world and the characters he's created, and to maintain their reality despite their manifest fiction.

So don't be ambitious. Don't reach for the stars. Instead, describe as simply as you can the quotidian textures of your imaginary world – and that world will spring to life with all the exuberance of felt reality.

LESSONS FROM THE GIUDECCA CANAL

Santa Maria del Rosario, on the Giudecca canal in Venice, is noted chiefly for its classical façade – enormous Corinthian pilasters support a heavy triangular pediment. It is an imposing presence on the shore of the canal, and must, at the time of its erection, have impressed both local Venetians and foreign visitors.

It was built on soil within metres of the shoreline. In order to support that daunting façade, the architect realised he would have to underpin the foundations of the church. The technology for doing so had been centuries in development.

First, bring in timber from the forests of Slovenia, Croatia and Montenegro. Then shape each trunk with adze and bowsaw. Each should be four metres or so in length, sharpened at one end, and solid through and through. Then hammer each of these into the mud and soil on which you intend to build. Upon this forest of stakes, erect a wooden platform – and upon *that*, build your particular vision of heaven.

Despite its extravagance, the façade of Santa Maria del Rosario, sometimes called I Gesuati, was a relatively modest undertaking. It required just 270 pilings to secure its foundation.

Much more ambitious was the church of Santa Maria della Salute, on the inner curve of Dorsoduro, at the entrance to the Grand Canal. Records kept at the time of its construction, just after a devastating plague had carried off a sizeable percentage of the city's residents in the early seventeenth century, show that over a million foundation stakes were driven into the mud and water.

When Venetians built their city upon the archipelago of islands dotting their lagoon, they didn't have a master plan. They worked one building at a time, skirting the natural tidal channels, driving in their wooden stakes on which to build their churches and their palazzi.

They were, essentially, opportunists: they took advantage of the natural contours of the islands. They consolidated their *fondamente* where it was possible – paying constant respect to the forces of the sea and the tides. And so, over the centuries, they built a jewel on the Adriatic so lustrous that it has beguiled artists, writers and merchants for a thousand years.

At our retreats each year, we try in a small way to help a number of writers navigate their way through the forest of options every writer encounters as she shapes the work she's engaged on. Some of these have devoted many hundreds of hours, and many thousands of words, to the task of realising on paper or the screen the image and the dream that drive their endeavours.

Some were struggling with the idea. Would it work, were these characters believable, was this story possible? Others had the story firmly fixed in their minds; their struggle was to tell it with verve and panache.

And the lesson that *I* kept learning and re-learning was that we all need to be opportunists, ready to take advantage of *this* imagined twist in the story, or *that* quirk of a character. We have to be ready to abandon the ideas that don't yield the drama we're after. We have to keep a wary eye constantly on the margins of what's possible and shore our stories up against the tides that threaten to undermine their credibility.

And over the course of, not centuries, but months, we're each of us capable of creating stories that will assert themselves in the imaginations of our readers with all the four-square solidity and confidence of a Santa Maria del Rosario.

TURN THE ACT OF WRITING INTO A CEREMONY

Just occasionally, when writing has become a burden – or perhaps, at that moment when you anticipate that it *will* become a burden – here's an idea...

It was inspired by immediate experience. When it occurred to me, it struck me at once as so right, as so obviously correct, that I couldn't resist sharing it with you.

But let me begin at the beginning. We rose, Trish and I, not at dawn, but at a civilised hour in our dark ground floor apartment off a narrow calle on the Giudecca Canal in Dorsoduro, Venice where we've come to prepare a new venue for our Venetian retreat later this year. Showered and dressed in our Saturday best we ventured forth in search of a barber our research had suggested we'd find on Rio Terra Foscarini a few metres from the Accademia Bridge on the Grand Canal.

There was no sign of the barber, although since so many shops in Venice do not bear signage proclaiming what services they offer, it's entirely possible we passed right by it.

"Never mind," I said, "let's have a cappuccino and a bite to eat."

There was a restaurant tucked in beside the bridge with tables immediately over the canal, and, as luck would have it, although every table appeared to be occupied, the proprietors opened a new section as we approached and we quickly nabbed the prime, corner table.

This is where we sit now, as I write these words. The bridge rises to my left. A constant stream of people pass over it from Dorsoduro into San Marco. On my right are the moorings of two gondolas. Soon after we placed our order, a party of South Africans settled in on one of the gondolas and with cries of delight and astonishment set off down the Grand Canal.

"I'm going to have to write my Monday Motivation," I said.

"Any idea what it's going to be about?" Trish asked.

I was about to shake my head when my idea occurred to me. Because here I was sitting in a prime spot overlooking one of the world's greatest prospects. It ranged from the wood and steel of Ponte dell'Accademia past a series of romantically seedy palazzos to the magisterial Santa Maria della Salute looming high above the mouth of the canal. The sky above me was that particular shade of pale blue found in Veronese's paintings. To the north, banks of bubbling cumulus are rising. (Heavy rain is forecast for this afternoon.)

Now, at noon, the bells of the Salute peal out across the city.

And writing this felt quite... ceremonial, almost sacramental.

My idea is this: when you feel, as I was saying before this long detour, that your enthusiasm is waning, your passion paling, or your stamina flagging, why not turn the act of writing into ceremony?

Clearly, it's not (always) possible to book a table at Bar Foscarini, but instead of dropping heavily into the slightly lopsided chair in your study, you could set up a small table outside in your garden, or on your balcony; you could arrange a rose in a vase and place it, just so, on the table; you could brew yourself a mug of that new Kenyan blend, or a cup of the most delicately scented jasmine tea; you could put something on that you feel good in after a vigorous shower or a languorous bath...

What you'd be doing, of course, is trying deliberately to cultivate an air of solemnity. Formality can be your friend, since it helps create both order and expectation. Sitting at your table, with your steaming cup at hand, and a blank screen (or page) before you, all you need to begin is an imagined voice in your ear that says:

"Let the wild rumpus begin."

NICE WORK, IF YOU CAN GET IT

I'm sitting in Campo San Polo in the coolth of the umbrellas of the Bar Cico, surrounded by a sprinkling of patrons. An elderly Italian man wrinkled and weather-worn sporting a fine set of long yellowing teeth, smokes a Camel at a corner table. His smoke wafts across to me and I tell myself this is Italy, where smoking is tolerated, so I tolerate it. His companion is a few years younger, in a spruce blue-and-white striped lounge shirt, gesticulating with the still smoking stub of a cigar. They are speaking in what I take to be the rather guttural patois of Venice.

It's just past ten in the morning, and the square is filling up as tourists (well, of course, I'm one myself, but since we are annual visitors, I'm starting to feel more like, if not a native, then a regular) filter in from the Rialto.

There are thin wisps of cloud across one quadrant of the sky, but for the rest it is that pure, undiluted blue we recognise from Veronese and Canaletto.

I'm sitting here, waiting for my Americano (my apologies, but cappuccinos in Italy are weak, luke-warm versions of what I consider the real thing) and thinking about the week ahead.

We have ten writers attending this year, most of whom come with a very specific writing project in mind. For those whose intentions are vaguer, we hope to tease out an idea – or a series of ideas – that they can explore.

What's really exciting from our point of view is the sense we have that we have absolutely *no* idea what's going to happen, in terms of this anthology of stories, over the next seven days. Life is more, but of course not totally, predictable – but stories aren't, or at least, shouldn't be.

In life, we're bound to each passing minute – in creative writing, whether fiction, non-fiction or film, we're free to make mighty leaps across days, weeks, years, even eons.

In life we're subject to the sort of random events that prompted Kurt Vonnegut to frame his phlegmatic lament: "So it goes," he wrote with a shrug.

In fiction, our characters trace carefully crafted trajectories that we design with very specific objectives in mind: to teach them… humility, acceptance, defiance, courage, love, surrender. Or, more simply, and if we're less morally inclined, we devise a series of incidents that are selected purely for their entertainment value – to our readers.

In life, we might sometimes feel there's no point to existence – in fiction, there's always point. (Unless you're a prisoner, I suppose, like Kafka's cockroach.)

To put it another way, in life we're not always certain what we want, and so often get distracted by the messages advertisers (or parents, or well-meaning friends) beam at us, but in fiction our characters *always* know what they want – although part of our purpose as their creators might sometimes be to demonstrate that what they *think* they want is not necessary what's good for them.

So what lies ahead of us are ten different paths, each bristling with options and possibilities, each full of purpose and meaning, each promising profound satisfaction.

It's nice work if you can get it.

SUCCUMBING TO THE INFINITE CHARMS OF VENICE

Years ago I sat at a table at All'Armonia, a restaurant perched on the lip of the quay overlooking the Giudecca Canal in Venice enjoying the late summer sun and a fine Campari spritz. While thus engaged, I contemplated the imposing edifice of Santa Maria del Rosario, a church built in the first half of the eighteenth century on a foundation of hundreds of stakes hammered into the mud flat on which Venice is built. Those thoughts appear in a piece you might just have read in this book.

Now, on a chilly day in late January, I found myself just a few metres down the *fondamenta*, at another restaurant, enjoying the last rays of a wintry sun. I was again looking at the church, and, inspired perhaps by the spritz on the table before me (I am, it seems, a creature of habit) my thoughts again turned to those timber foundations.

Hundreds of stakes, each four metres or so long, hammered painstakingly into the ooze. Each of these stakes on its own did not provide much support. I dare say that *dozens* of them would, likewise, not have done the trick.

But when they stood side by side in their seried ranks, each supporting those flanking it, and being supported in their turn by their neighbours, they were able, collectively, to support the enormous weight of the church built on top of them. Look up a picture of Santa Maria, rising high above the other buildings of the neighbourhood. It must weigh thousands of tons.

When a writer sets out to create a world – or a character – she does so just as the builders of Santa Maria did, by hammering in one stake, one pile, one detail at a time. None of these on its own is enough to sustain the world being evoked, but together they're up to the task.

By the time they're all in place, the illusion is complete – and the foundations of your world invisible.

Looking at Santa Maria del Rosario – or any of the hundreds of other wondrous buildings here, some much larger and elaborate than this particular church – you're not aware of the legerdemain that underpins them and the scrupulous attention paid to the engineering.

What you admire is the whole, that extraordinary classical building which houses some of the most admired paintings in all of Venice by Tiepolo, Piazzetta, Ricci, and Tintoretto.

Get the underpinning right, and you can do whatever strikes your fancy on that foundation.

As I write these words, the noon chorus of bells sounds out across the city, and I suspect that I, like hundreds before me, have succumbed to the infinite charms of Venice. Perhaps I'm looking for writerly analogies where none exist, simply because La Serenissima is so inspiring.

Happy writing wherever you are.

PEOPLE-WATCHING IN VENICE

Writers *observe*. Their observations serve as the foundations on which characters are built and stories developed. Our retreats here in Venice give me unparalleled opportunities to observe people going about their business.

I set up my observation post at a café on a nearby canal. I am armed with a notebook, a pen, and a pint of Birra Moretti. Here are my notes:

A blonde in shocking pink pants herds her family – a husband, their eleven-year-old daughter, a baby in a pram, and a third child, a girl of six or seven – into a sullen group. The back-drop, carefully curated by the mother, is an elegant marble bridge. She gives instructions to the younger daughter, and hands her her cell phone.

While her daughter adopts the universal pose of photographers everywhere, finger poised above the button, she, the mother that is, arranges the family tableau: first, she whirls the baby's pushchair around so that the infant is sure to feature in the picture, then she passes her arm around her impassive husband, poses prettily, tilts her hip, bends one leg, and smiles. The younger girl dutifully takes the photograph. The mother checks it, approves it, and briskly waves her posse on.

A water taxi driver, standing in the cockpit of his sleek cream taxi, is having a long conversation with a gondolier. Their boats are moored in a twist in the canal Rio del Malcanton. It's lunch time. They speak very loudly, having calibrated their voices to carry over the roar of engines and the slap of waves against prow. The engines are quiet now, and the waves quiescent – but their voices remain strident and very Venetian.

An elderly American, large and noisy, sits at the table alongside me with his more or less silent wife. He orders, loudly, an Americano, with a double shot. Stubble covers his cheeks and throat. His wife says nothing while he drinks his coffee, and then suggests that they "move on". They do.

Our waitress, an inscrutable Italian woman, wears an apron with the words, LIFE IS GOOD, printed across the front.

It's not the physical characteristics of these people that strike me so much as the way in which they walk. This one approaching now from the left walks with a confident, long-legged stride; this one scissors along at speed; that one glides, appearing hardly to touch the ground; that pair of new arrivals trudges along doggedly, each hauling two or three wheeled suitcases, clearly on their way to their lodgings after an exhausting journey. And here's a man who strolls along insouciantly, his hands in his pockets. He's in no hurry, either on this Thursday afternoon or, perhaps, in life.

I briefly play a game spotting celebrities: at the last table in my café sits John Cleese with an Aperol spritz. A rather rickety version of one of those British politicians whose names I never remember, in not this, but the last, cabinet, or was it the one before (it's so difficult to keep track) hobbles past. And here, by god, comes Cameron Diaz, wearing not just her usual sly grin of amusement, but a pearl tiara! And she and her partner, an indifferent consort with torn jeans and a tee-shirt, take the table besides mine. They speak English – but clearly for both of them, it is their second, or perhaps even third language. He could be Italian, she could be Russian. They order an Aperol spritz for her, and a cappuccino for him. She photographs the canal with her spritz in the foreground. And then a miniature Michael Jackson passes by...

Across the road from me, two women and a man wait in attendance at a Jehovah's Witness stand. Passers-by who appear to be approaching them are greeted with joyous smiles. Most are alarmed and veer away, but one Italian family, six strong, stops to talk. My guess is that they're not prospects but converts. The stands at which the Witnesses stand are laden with booklets and adorned with posters. The first poses the legitimate question: WAS LIFE CREATED? in English. The second is in Italian: COSA VUOL DIRE AVERE SUCCESSO NELLA VITA? What does it mean to succeed in life? Also a good question. And the third is the killer: CORSO BIBLICO GRATUITO. Free bible course, at which, presumably, the answers to the first two questions will be provided.

A man from Salento Bakery – where earlier this morning I spent a couple of hours working on a project and drinking three cups of delicious cappuccino – his tummy preceding him, walks past with two bulging paper carrier bags prominently branded. I assume he's delivering baked goods to a customer.

On a wall diagonally opposite me a fragment of graffiti encourages me to UNLOCK YOUR SOUL. Sitting here bathed in the warming balm of the autumnal sun, with my Birra Moretti at hand, I feel, for a moment, complete. My soul is indeed unlocked.

And, perhaps, what's even more satisfying is the fact that I have a complete new cast of characters ready to populate the next fiction I turn my hand to.

TIME AND THE PANICKING WRITER

Science tells us that at the normal speeds at which we live our lives, time passes as the clock ticks – at an invariable rate. As our velocity approaches the speed of light, Einstein said, time slows down. And yet we don't need to consult Einstein's equations to agree that our subjective experience of time can vary enormously, as even a child is aware.

As writers, as I've pointed out before, we have the power to manipulate time on the page. We can speed it up, and we can slow it down to suit our dramatic purposes.

Here's something that happened during a recent writing retreat in Croatia (an experimental add-on to the Venetian retreat) that brought home to me just how much can happen in the space of seconds – and how, if a writer were to render it in words, he'd have to slow time down to make sense of the drama.

The mentoring team lodged in a house that neighboured the villa in which the retreaters luxuriated. Every morning, we drove up to the main house to join our mentees for breakfast.

Our house stood on a fairly steep slope. A gravel driveway ran up to the front door. On the morning in question, I took my place on the back seat of the van, leaving the sliding door open.

Neither the driver nor I bothered to buckle up because our journey was such a short one.

The driver – no names here, to protect the innocent – started the engine and put the van into reverse.

Now you need to know a couple of facts about both the vehicle and the driveway. The vehicle was a Mercedes Vito. One of its features is a "handbrake" situated in the footwell. It is, in short, not a handbrake at all. So arrayed across the footwell are four pedals: the "handbrake", the accelerator, the clutch and the brake.

My driver wasn't accustomed to this unusual feature of the vehicle.

And as for the driveway, well, as I said, it was fairly steep. It ran down to a gravel road that led off to the left where it joined the main road. If you'd asked me what there was at the foot of the slope, I'd have said, Mmm, perhaps a couple of bushes and a low stone wall.

But back to the action. As I said, the driver started the engine and put the vehicle into reverse. Actually, later, he confessed that perhaps the reverse gear probably hadn't engaged at all.

And we started rolling down the slope.

"I can't find the brake," he said.

"What?"

The speed of the van crunching over the gravel increased.

The driver turned to me. His face was white, his eyes wide, his nostrils flaring. "I can't find the brake!"

By now we seemed to be hurtling down that slope. He couldn't find the brake? How was that possible? Oh my God, we were only metres from our front door, how could we have found ourselves in this *impossible* situation so quickly?

"Push the brake!" I yelled.

"I can't, I can't, I can't find it..."

"Push *anything*!"

I braced myself for what I was sure would be the crunch of our rear into the wall behind us. An image flashed through my mind of me being thrown out through the open door, of...

And then our tyres dug into the gravel, pebbles flew out behind us and we slithered to an abrupt stop.

For a moment, there was utter silence.

"I found the brake," the driver said.

We got out of the van and stumbled to the back of the van to see how close we'd come to the wall.

And discovered that there wasn't a wall at all – just a single rusty chain looped from one flimsy garden stake to another, and beyond that... a three metre drop into an open field.

We'd stopped fifty centimetres from the brink. Had the driver stamped down on the brake a split second later – or chosen the wrong pedal to push – we'd have plunged over the edge into the abyss with who knows what consequences to the two of us.

The entire experience lasted four or five seconds. Our panic lasted for a fraction of that. I've just read this account of the incident. It took me two minutes and ten seconds.

I think even Einstein would have been impressed.

ATTEND, OBSERVE, SPECULATE AND IMAGINE

Coming to Venice and working with an unrepentant gang of writers reminds you of some of the fundamentals of creative writing. Why? Because for a week or two you do nothing but talk about writing and its challenges, listen to writers read bits of their writing, and celebrate the very particular joy that writing inspires.

You can't help but find yourself rummaging about in the cellar of inspiration for the key precepts of the craft.

The city itself positively demands that you pay attention to your environment: the graffitied walls; the intricate iron- and woodwork of windows and lintels, of balustrades and bridges; the infinitely varied colours of the glittering canals, sparkling in the sun, leaden under heavy cloud, dimpled in the rain. Your eye is drawn to the tawdry splendour of mouldering palazzos, the burnished gleam of water taxis, the ever-present flutter of pigeons at your feet, or making an opportunistic lunge for the croissant on your plate, just inches from your writing hand.

Observation is the foundation stone of writing practice – but it demands more than a sharp eye and a ready notebook.

One layer down from seeing and recording, is interpreting. You see a pedestrian strolling past and you deduce from some detail of his appearance – a splash of paint on his sleeve, perhaps, a daub of colour on his forehead – that he is a painter, not of walls and ceilings but of canvasses. Perhaps he is one of those sometimes to be seen at work on their easels on perches along the Grand Canal.

You see a young woman with a laurel wreath in her hair talking earnestly to an older woman, and you intuit that she is a student, just graduated, talking to a proud parent. Perhaps they're on their way to Harry's Bar for a celebratory Bellini.

These speculations yield the seeds of stories and of characters that are meat and potatoes to any writer. Sow a few of these seeds in the fertile soil of your imagination and, hey presto! a narrative could emerge.

The dreaming city promotes the posing of hypothetical questions concerning both its present and a past that seems more accessible here than in any other city I've ever visited. Walking through Campo Santa Margarita, you hear the spritely strains of a piece of music emerging from a church. You recognise it's a piece by Vivaldi who lived and died in this city in the seventeenth and eighteenth centuries.

You pause, take a seat on a red bench, and listen carefully. Four centuries ago, those same notes, played by identical instruments, might have been audible from this very spot. Your thoughts dwell on who that lover of music might have been, what role he played in the city, where he was coming from and where he was going...

Perhaps his ghost – and the ghosts of countless others – are summoned back into half-life whenever the music of Vivaldi, or Monteverdi, or Cavalli is played. Could any of them have imagined, so many centuries later, that their music would continue to waft through the Venetian air, inspiring some, entertaining others and quite possibly irritating those for whom the music is a distraction from the more urgent routines of day and doing.

And what of three or four centuries hence, when the stub of the great San Marco clocktower protrudes from the ever-rising waters of the sea, when the lagoon has been swallowed by the Adriatic, and when all that remains of the city are a few ruined church spires, and the upper floors of a handful of palazzi?

In the grandest of those palazzi, one of the few Venetians left is standing at the great window of the piano nobile, looking out over the surging tide, playing with singular and passionate focus a Vivaldi cello sonata. Behind him are ranged all the ghosts of the once vibrant city, crowding in to hear this last performance.

Paying attention, observing, speculating and imagining. These are the strings we at our Venice retreat draw our bow across, producing stories that we trust – and hope – will delight our readers.

THE ENDLESS CURRENT

We're back in Bedford now for a final rumination. Our voyage for the moment is over. Trish and I sit on the deck of Impatience, glasses of Chablis within reach, watching the evening settle over Priory Marina.

I'm struck by how the journey we've shared through these pages mirrors the voyages we've taken on England's waterways. Just as rivers flow inexorably toward the sea, carrying all manner of flotsam and jetsam, so too has this collection gathered fragments of insight, observation, and experience along its course.

When I began these Monday Writing Motivations all those years ago at Trish's urging, I had little conception of where the current would take us. Like our first hesitant journeys on Patience, we set out with a rough idea of direction but remained open to the unexpected vistas, the curious encounters, the occasional mishaps that give texture to any journey worth taking.

What strikes me now, looking back over these collected thoughts, is how consistently the water has served as both medium and metaphor. Not merely a backdrop for our adventures, but a teacher with endless lessons to impart. The deceptive stillness of the lake concealing currents beneath; the persistence required to navigate a flight of leaking locks; the patience needed to spot a kingfisher's flash of azure – all of these have their counterparts in the writer's craft.

I'm reminded of that afternoon on the Thames when the river ran so fast beneath us that we could hardly control our course. Writing can be like that – sometimes we're swept along by ideas that carry us beyond our intended destination. Other times, like our days marooned at Osney Lock with the Red Boards up, we find ourselves frustratingly becalmed, waiting for conditions to change before we can continue.

Perhaps what matters most is paying attention, keeping our eyes open. The greatest power we have as writers is in our observation – in noticing that "corrugated smile" of a cowrie shell, as Helen Scales so perfectly described it. This reminds me that the specific, the textural, the precisely observed detail is the currency of our craft. Whether it's a heron's patience as she stands for long hours in the shallows watching and waiting, a Canada goose's territorial rage, or the rhythmic clangour of Venetian bells echoing across the Giudecca Canal, it's in the details that the universal is revealed.

And what of you, dear reader, who has accompanied us on these waterborne musings? I hope you've found something worth keeping – a phrase that resonated, an observation that illuminated, a thought that provoked.

Writing, like cruising the canals, is ultimately a shared experience. The narrowboat passing in the opposite direction with a friendly wave; the lock-keeper's nugget of local wisdom; the fellow writer's struggle with character or plot - these connections enrich our journeys and remind us we're not alone on the water.

I realise now that what began as "little meditations" has become something more: a chart of sorts, mapping not just the waterways of England and the canals of Venice, but the deeper currents of creativity that flow through all of us who put words on paper.

The John Bunyan, the tourist wide-beam that moors on our lake, passes by, filled with pensioners on what seems to be a birthday jaunt. The tillerman sounds his horn to alert traffic on the river (there's hardly ever any) that they're about to emerge from the marina. The passing of the boat reveals our swans making their evening round. Night is drawing in. But tomorrow brings another journey, another blank page, another chance to cast off and see where the current takes us.

And isn't that, after all, why we write? To set our fragile barques upon that sea of possibility, not always knowing our destination but trusting in the voyage itself to reveal what matters most.

So let us end as we began – on the water, watching for herons, listening to the wind in the willows, feeling the gentle rocking of words beneath us, and always, always curious about what lies around the next bend in the river.

THANK YOU FOR READING

Thank you for joining me on this journey. I hope that the words and lessons within these pages have inspired you as much as the waterways themselves have inspired me. I'd love to hear your thoughts.

Please leave a review

If you found something valuable in these pages, please consider leaving a short review on the platform where you bought the book, or on Goodreads. Reviews help other writers discover books that might just change their creative lives – and they mean the world to indie authors.

WANT MORE WRITING INSPIRATION?

If you've enjoyed *Waterlines*, I invite you to join my Monday Writing Motivation community. Each Monday, I send a short, thoughtful reflection on the writing life – designed to spark ideas and keep you writing.

Subscribe to my Monday Writing Motivations here:

www.richardbeynonbooks.com

CRAFT, CREATIVITY AND THE WRITING LIFE

Waterlines is part of the *Craft, Creativity and the Writing Life* series — a collection of books designed to support writers at every stage of the journey. Each book explores a different facet of the writing life, from creative resilience to narrative structure to the writer's role in the world.

Each title is accompanied by a practical workbook, featuring prompts, questions, and exercises inspired by the essays — so you can turn insight into writing practice.

Want to be notified when the next volumes and workbooks are released?

Sign up to receive notifications and weekly Monday Writing Motivations:

www.richardbeynonbooks.com

Books in the series

Waterlines: Writing Lessons from a Life Afloat Aboard his narrowboat, Richard Beynon finds a masterclass in creativity. This collection of essays reveals how the world around you can inspire skill and passion, helping you master your craft without losing the joy of storytelling.

Inside Story: A Writer's Guide to Crafting Compelling Stories Move beyond theory and into the architecture of great stories. This book explores the fundamentals of narrative, from creating tension and crafting authentic characters to building scenes that hook readers and keep them turning pages.

A Dance in the Writing Room: What It Means to Be a Writer Go deeper than the craft and into the soul of a writer. Through personal anecdotes and philosophical insights, this collection addresses the inner challenges of the writing life – from sustaining courage and overcoming doubt to finding the alchemy of inspiration.

The Companion Workbooks

Book 1: *Waterlines Companion Workbook* Transform the wisdom of *Waterlines* into daily practice with this hands-on companion. Filled with exercises and prompts, it helps you generate story ideas, sharpen your instincts, and get you writing more fluently than ever.

Book 2: *Inside Story Companion Workbook* Go beyond theory and master the art of storytelling through practice. This workbook offers concrete exercises with clear objectives that teach you to build compelling narratives, from crafting a perfect opening to developing authentic characters.

Book 3: *A Dance in the Writing Room Companion Workbook* Strengthen both your writing and your writer's soul with this guide to the psychological landscape of the creative life. It's a collection of exercises that build courage, confidence, and the resilience needed to sustain your writing journey.

ABOUT RICHARD BEYNON

I am a storyteller whose career was launched when, at the age of seven, I contracted polio and struck a bargain with my hospital wardmates: they would strap my brace onto my leg – and I would tell them stories.

Since then, I've spent my life telling stories in countless forms as a journalist, and writing for the page and the screen. I've written over 1200 scripts of drama and comedy, led dozens of writers' rooms, and served as head writer on some of South Africa's most popular soaps.

In 2006, I co-founded All About Writing with novelist Jo-Anne Richards. Together with our partner, Trish Urquhart, we've helped thousands of writers take their stories seriously – many of whom have gone on to publish award-winning work.

For fifteen years, I lived for months each year on my narrowboat, Patience, navigating the rivers and canals of England and Wales. From that watery vantage, I wrote more than 500 motivational essays about writing and life.

Now based on a houseboat on the River Great Ouse in Bedford, UK, I continue to write my Monday Writing Motivations - delivered fresh every Monday. If you'd like a weekly dose of inspiration, please subscribe at www.richardbeynonbooks.com

Connect with me:

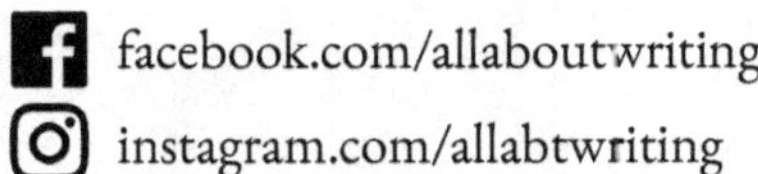

HOW I WORK WITH WRITERS

Through All About Writing, I offer a range of services to help writers at every stage of their journey. I believe that every writer can find their voice and tell their story with confidence, and I'm here to help you do that.

My services include:

- **Mentoring and Story Doctoring:** One-on-one guidance for writers working on fiction, creative non-fiction, and screenplays. I help with everything from initial idea development to polishing a final draft.
- **Workshops and Retreats:** I host in-person weekend workshops in the UK and with my partner Jo-Anne Richards, an annual writing retreat in Venice.
- **Courses:** All About Writing offers a wide selection of online courses and resources. Our flagship Creative Writing Course is designed to teach all the skills you need to write a book – fiction or non-fiction.
- **Ghostwriting and Collaboration:** For individuals with a story to tell but not the time or desire to write it themselves.

To learn more please visit the All About Writing website

www.allaboutwritingcourses.com

BIBLIOGRAPHY AND RESOURCES

First Voyage
Object Lessons: The Paris Review Presents the Art of the Short Story – edited by Lorin and Sadie Stein
From Pitch to Publication: Everything You Need To Know To Get Your Novel Published – Carole Blake
The Fun Stuff and Other Essays – James Wood
Britain by the Book – a curious tour of our literary landscape – Oliver Tearle
The Right to Write: An Invitation and Initiation into the Writing Life – Julia Cameron
Brave Lotus Flower Rides the Dragon – Tracy Todd
His Dark Materials, The Book of Dust and The Sally Lockhart series – Philip Pullman
Chocolat – Joanne Harris
Full Dark House (Bryant & May Book 1) – Christopher Fowler

Second Voyage
The Hero with a Thousand Faces – Joseph Campbell
Our Mutual Friend – Charles Dickens
Songs of Ice and Fire – George R.R. Martin
The Hobbit by J.R.R. Tolkien
The Hero's Journey Course
www.allaboutwritingcourses.com/heros_journey

Third Voyage
On Writing: A Memoir of the Craft – Stephen King
My Brilliant Friend – Elena Ferrante
My Struggle – Karl Ove Knausgaard
Spirals in Time: The Secret Life and Curious Afterlife of Seashells – Dr Helen Scales

The River Great Ouse, Bedford
High Flight – John Gillespie Magee
www.poetryfoundation.org/poems/157986/high-flight-627d3cfb1e9b7
The Magician – Colm Tóibín

The River Great Ouse and Other Seas
Ulysses – James Joyce
Atomic Habits – James Clear
The Sign of the Four – Arthur Conan-Doyle;

The Garden – Andrew Marvell
www.poetryfoundation.org/poems/44682/the-garden-56d223dec2ced

Meanwhile the mind, from pleasure less,
Withdraws into its happiness;
The mind, that ocean where each kind
Does straight its own resemblance find,
Yet it creates, transcending these,
Far other worlds, and other seas;
Annihilating all that's made
To a green thought in a green shade.

The Wind in the Willows – Kenneth Grahame

Venice

Venice Writing Retreat
www.allaboutwritingcourses.com/venice-retreat
Slaughterhouse 5 – Kurt Vonnegut
Metamorphosis – Franz Kafka

www.ingramcontent.com/pod-product-compliance
Lightning Source LLC
Chambersburg PA
CBHW050614190726
48283CB00007B/2420

9781918023015